TOWARD UNDERSTANDING ROMANS

An Introduction and Exegetical Translation

By Boyce W. Blackwelder, M.A., Th.D.

AUTHOR OF

Light from the Greek New Testament

AND

Toward Understanding Paul

THE WARNER PRESS

ANDERSON, INDIANA

To
ALICE LELA

whose life exemplifies
God's kind of righteousness

Preface

Paul's Epistle to the Romans is without doubt the most important theological document ever written. It is not only the longest but also the most systematic and comprehensive presentation of the Apostle's thought which has come down to us. Hunter has suggested that an appropriate subtitle for it would be "The Gospel According to St. Paul."[1]

Romans has formed the background of the great historic statements of Christian doctrine, and all serious theologians of the present day realize its significance as a delineation of the New Testament message. Although the literature on Romans is already vast, the Epistle is so challenging and inexhaustible that every effort given to its interpretation is fruitful.

Several years ago I was requested by the editorial department of Warner Press to prepare a translation of Romans, using reasonable freedom in bringing out the implications of the Greek vocabulary and syntax. The original plan was to publish the rendition chapter by chapter in the *Gospel Trumpet*. However, as the work progressed, we thought it might be more helpful to readers if we combined with the translation a brief introduction to the Epistle and presented the material in book form.

The translation was made from the Greek text edited by Professor Eberhard Nestle, fourth edition, 1904 (London: British and Foreign Bible Society, 1934). The Nestle text is the resultant of a collation of three of the principal recensions of the Greek New Testament which appeared in the latter half of the nineteenth century—those of

[1]Archibald M. Hunter, *Introducing the New Testament*, p. 91.

Tischendorf, Westcott-Hort, and Bernhard Weiss. In checking variant readings, I also used for reference Erwin Nestle's *Novum Testamentum Graece* (Stuttgart: Privilegierte Württembergische Bibelanstalt, 1932), and Augustinus Merk's *Novum Testamentum Graece et Latine* (Rome: Pontifical Biblical Institute, 1944), both of which have helpful critical apparatus.

It is the responsibility of a translator to strive for grammatical precision. What reliable scholars, after long years of painstaking research, have decided is the best text deserves the utmost respect and should be rendered as accurately as possible. Decisions should be reached on exegetical grounds and not on the basis of dogmatic considerations.

There is a case in point in Romans 5:1. The manuscript evidence favors *echōmen* (hortatory subjunctive) meaning *"let us have* peace," rather than *echomen* (indicative) *"we have* peace." A number of commentators are sure that the sense of the passage calls for the indicative. Reasoning from Paul's theology in general, and from the implications of the immediate context, that peace with God is the result of justification by faith and not of personal effort after justification, they conclude that Paul actually dictated *echomen* but that his amanuensis thought he had said *echōmen* inasmuch as there is little if any difference in the pronunciation of the two terms.

For the exegete who respects the strongest manuscript authority, there is no argument. He takes it as *echōmen*. But there is really no theological problem in the passage, for *echōmen* is the present subjunctive, *"let us continue to have* peace with God." Paul is exhorting believers to maintain the peace which is the result of having been declared righteous by faith.

An understanding of Greek does not remove all the difficulties of translation. There are times when a grammarian exhausts his resources and still cannot be positive about a rendering. For example, the verb *proechometha* in Romans 3:9 is such a problem. Should we treat it as middle, *"Have we advantage for ourselves?"* or as passive, *"Are we surpassed?"* The grammar allows either interpretation, but the translator must make a decision. I have rendered it as middle, which seems a bit more in harmony with Paul's discussion in the immediate context.

Translation is far more than presenting literal English equivalents for Greek words. The Greek language is very expressive and conveys many shades of meaning and variations of thought which cannot be carried over in their fullness to English. The same Greek word cannot always be rendered by the same English word. In different contexts the same Greek term may have different, and sometimes even contrasting or opposite, meanings. Translation is filling in the total picture, as best we can, with the ideas contributed by the Greek modes, tenses, cases, emphatic pronouns, the use or nonuse of the article, and the like. And there are certain idiomatic expressions which must be rendered appropriately. Thus from all the syntactical elements an interpreter seeks to impart the thought of an original writer and to convey, at least to some extent, the force of the author's emotions and literary style.

I have sought to indicate something of the elasticity of Greek conjunctions. The most frequent use of *gar* is illative, but in traditional translations this meaning has been overworked. There are contexts in which *gar* does not introduce a reason, but is only explanatory, and I have rendered it "now" (e.g., Rom. 2:12, 25; 4:2). In such instances it could be rendered, "to explain further." There are clear instances of *gar* as an emphatic particle. I render it "emphatically" in Romans 4:9. "Actually" seems appropriate in 1:26; 2:14; 3:20; 7:15; 8:18; 9:19; "indeed" in 1:16; 2:24; 4:15; 5:6; 6:7; 8:3, 15, 19; 9:15; 10:4, 12; 15:27; "in fact" in 2:28; "certainly" in 1:18; 5:13; 7:22; 14:18; 15:3; "of course" in 10:2; "why" in 5:7; 11:1. The conjunction *oun* commonly has an inferential meaning, as in 14:12; but sometimes it is adversative (cf. "however" in 2:26). With *ara* it denotes emphasis in 9:16; 14:12, 19.

Paul frequently uses the expression *mē genoito,* an optative of wishing, which means literally, *May it not happen!* It conveys a very strong emphatic negative idea. Paul employs it to express a vigorous denial and to repudiate without qualification a false notion or inference. The "God forbid" of the King James Version brings out the force of the Greek idiom. I have used several different expressions to render *mē genoito,* somewhat for variety and also in an effort to approach the precise meaning implied by each context, e.g., "By no means!" (3:4); "Not at all!" 3:6, 31; 7:13); "Away with the thought!" (6:2); "Certainly not!" (6:15; 7:7; 11:1, 11); "Unthinkable!" (9:14).

One of the most versatile terms in Romans is *nomos* (law). Both with and without the article it has a variety of significations. Paul sometimes employs *nomos* in the generic sense to indicate everything in the whole realm of law. No doubt the Mosaic enactments, in which Paul was brought up, had been for him the embodiment of law. Certainly they represented the divine requirements which demanded exact obedience. But when Paul states, as he does so often in Romans, that by means of law no person can be justified, he is saying that there is no efficacy in any kind of legislation, whether it be the specific statutes revealed from Mount Sinai or otherwise. Although in many instances in Romans *nomos* without the article denotes "law in general," there are passages in which this construction refers to the "Law of Moses." But when *nomos* indicates the Mosaic system, the anarthrous construction refers to that system not essentially as Mosaic but to its character as law.

Many passages in Romans are very difficult to translate. Quite often, in order to express the Greek idiom in comparable English, it was necessary to resort to paraphrase. Brackets enclose words inserted in an effort to convey meanings which are implicit, if not explicit, in the Greek text. In some instances explanatory footnotes have been used to indicate the syntactical basis for a rendering.

I wish to acknowledge my grateful indebtedness to Dr. Julius R. Mantey, member of the faculty of Northern Baptist Theological Seminary 1925-1960, and now Professor Emeritus of New Testament Interpretation; to Dr. Louis F. Gough of Warner Pacific College; and to Dr. Adam W. Miller of Anderson College and Theological Seminary for their kindness in reading the typescript and offering pertinent suggestions.

—Boyce W. Blackwelder

Erie, Pennsylvania

Contents

PAUL'S EPISTLE TO THE ROMANS

PART I
INTRODUCTION

CHAPTER I

Ancient Rome

Rome is one of the oldest cities in the world. Its Seven Hills have long been famous, and there are many interesting aspects of its legendary and authentic history. Majestic remains, which are visible symbols of the culture of the ancient city, may be seen even today in the modern capital.

Rome is of special interest to students of the New Testament because it was the ruling power of the world into which Christianity came. Augustus, who was monarch at the time of Jesus' birth (Luke 2:1), exercised supreme control over the Empire for nearly half a century (27 B.C.–A.D. 14). Tiberius, the stepson of Augustus, was emperor (A.D. 14-37) during the Palestinian ministry and crucifixion of Jesus (Luke 3:1). It was Tiberius' image and title which were stamped on the silver coin (denarius) which Jesus used in answering the Pharisees and Herodians when they sought to trap him with the question about tribute to Caesar (Matt. 22:15-22). In the reign of Claudius (A.D. 41-54), the early church began its great period of missionary expansion, of which the journeys of Paul were the most impressive feature. Nero (A.D. 54-68) was the first Roman emperor who persecuted the Christians.[1] It was to the church at Rome that Paul wrote his most extensive epistle. In Rome he was imprisoned, probably twice, and in that vicinity his martyrdom took place. The traditional

---

[1]In July, A.D. 64, great fires destroyed two thirds of the city of Rome. In order to divert from himself the suspicion of having started the conflagration, Nero placed the blame on the Christians and bitter persecution began against them.

spot where the great Apostle was beheaded by the sword is the Three Fountains on the Ostian road, outside the walls of the imperial metropolis.

LONG HISTORY

Not much is known about the beginnings of Rome. The oldest accounts are intermingled with so much myth that few statements can be regarded as having a basis in fact. Among the legends which tell of the founding of the city is the story of the Trojan warrior Aeneas, son of Anchises and Venus, goddess of love and beauty. Then there is the fable of Romulus and Remus, twin sons of the war god Mars and the vestal virgin Rhea Silvia, daughter of Numitor, king of Alba.

The Romans fixed 753 B.C. as the year of the city's founding, and they dated events from that year, but there is evidence that the site of Rome was inhabited long before that time. Archaeological discoveries indicate that as early as 1000 B.C. primitive communities existed on several of the highest hills, including the Palatine, the Capitoline, and the Esquiline. The first residents were probably Latins, Etruscans, and Sabines.

The history of ancient Rome falls into three general divisions: the regal period (753-510 B.C.), the years of the Republic (509-27 B.C.), and the era of the Empire (27 B.C. —A.D. 476). By 275 B.C. Rome had gained control of all Italy and was one of the two strongest dominions of the western Mediterranean. Her rival was Carthage, at that time the foremost maritime power of the world. Situated in what is now Tunisia, in North Africa, Carthage commanded an empire which extended from Sicily to the Strait of Gibraltar.

In the Punic Wars (265-146 B.C.), Rome defeated the Carthaginians, took their Mediterranean islands, and made Spain a Roman province. In 196 B.C. Titus Flamininus, the Roman envoy, declared the liberation of all the Greek states. In 190 B.C. Antiochus the Great, king of Syria, who had invaded Asia Minor and advanced into Greece, was defeated by the Roman general Scipio the Elder at Magnesia, ancient city of Ionia, and forced to surrender his possessions in Europe and Asia Minor. In the middle of the second century B.C. the Greeks rose in revolt, but they were crushed by the massive military might of Rome. In 146 B.C. Corinth, the last center of Greek strength, was completely destroyed by the Roman commander Lucius Mummius.

Thus fifty years after gaining the ascendancy in the West by defeating Hannibal's Carthaginian armies at Zama in 202 B.C., Rome had also become the most powerful state in the East, and within a century and a quarter had developed from a land power, which dominated only the Italian peninsula, into a world empire. During this period of conquest the Romans made marked cultural advances. As they came into contact with Greek refinement in southern Italy, and as they expanded to the east, they embraced many ideas from the art, literature, and philosophy of the older civilization.

In 59 B.C. Julius Caesar invaded Gaul and, after ten years of continuous fighting, subdued the entire country from the Rhine River to the Atlantic Ocean. When he returned from his Gallic victory in 49 B.C., Caesar became the sole ruler of Rome, thus bringing to an end the Roman republic and ushering in the age of the Caesars.

After the assassination of the great Roman in 44 B.C., Octavian (63 B.C.—A.D. 14), son of Attia, the daughter of

Caesar's sister Julia, gained control. In 27 B.C., Octavian became the first emperor of Rome, and the Latin title "Augustus" (meaning majestic or exalted, a term heretofore used only of the gods) was conferred upon him by the senate. His control of the army carried the title of Imperator (signifying director or commander, and basis of our word emperor), and he called himself *Princeps* (which means "the first," i.e., the "first citizen"). Octavian ruled under republican forms, and he shared his administrative responsibilities with the senate, but the power of the state was invested in one person whose word was law.

The immediate successors of Augustus added slightly to Roman territory (at its widest extent the Empire stretched approximately three thousand miles from east to west, and two thousand miles from north to south), but after the reign of Marcus Aurelius (A.D. 161-180) the decline began. Diocletian (A.D. 284-305), and Constantine The Great (A.D. 306-337) instituted military and administrative reforms which delayed the disintegration. Finally, weakened by corruption from within and attacked by enemies from without, the Empire began to crumble. In A.D. 395 it was broken into two divisions, the Eastern or Byzantine, and the Western. In A.D. 476 the Empire of the West was overthrown by Odoacer, a Goth, who captured Rome and became king of Italy. The Byzantine Empire (also called the Eastern, Greek, or Later Roman Empire) lasted until the fall of its capital, Constantinople, in the year 1453.

PREPARATION FOR CHRISTIANITY

Three civilizations played significant roles in bringing about "the fullness of the time" (Gal. 4:4) preparatory to the rise of Christianity. The Hebrews gave to the world the Old Testament Scriptures which emphasized monotheism and enunciated the prophecies of the coming Messiah. The Hellenes provided the Greek language which was the best instrument of human expression ever devised. Carried across the Mediterranean lands by the conquering armies of Alexander the Great, Koinē (commonly spoken) Greek became the language widely used during the Greco-Roman period. Thus a world-speech was available for the oral and written dissemination of the gospel. Rome's chief legacy was in the realm of law and public administration, and in the work of skilled engineers.

In looking more closely at the background which the Roman Empire provided for the coming of Christianity, we note the following contributions:

1. *Universal order and tranquility.* The reign of Augustus marked the beginning of the famous *pax Romana* (Roman peace). The Romans had ceased their own civil wars, and had ended the internal strife of cities and conflicts among the nations. From Britain to Babylonia, and from the Danube and the Black Sea to the Nile valley the world was at rest. Many peoples had never known administrative peace until the days of Roman supremacy. Under the Empire, whole provinces were free from war for generations.

The New Testament speaks of *pasan tēn oikoumenēn* meaning "the whole inhabited earth" (Luke 2:1), denoting the domain ruled by Caesar Augustus. The extensive sweep of Roman sovereignty gave the Christian missionaries an assurance of safety as they went forth to declare the gospel to strange and sometimes unfriendly peoples.

2. *Impetus to travel and trade.* In order to govern the areas which she had conquered, Rome built a massive system of roads. These thoroughfares were the best means of

communication the world had ever seen until the era of railroads and modern highways. Mountains were tunneled, streams and valleys were bridged, and marshes were spanned by viaducts of masonry. The roads were usually not more than fifteen feet wide, but they were smooth, being paved with slabs of rock which were bound together by an excellent cement. The roads, bridges, and aqueducts were constructed so skillfully that many of them have endured until the present day.

The first of the famous Roman roads was the *Via Appia,* or Appian Way (Acts 28:15), built in 312 B.C. It connected the capital with Capua and southern Italy. Other roads were built, spreading out eastward and northward, like the spokes of a wheel. In time the farthest limits of the Empire were traversed by a network of highways. Thus the saying, "All roads lead to Rome," was literally true. Not only did soldiers and the imperial posts move along the thoroughfares, but when the *pax Romana* opened the door for extensive travel, streams of traders and caravans filled the inviting roadways.

The Mediterranean Sea, whose shores were encircled by the Roman dominions, was of course an important means of transportation. In 67 B.C. Pompey cleared the previously formidable pirates from its waters and made the shipping lanes safe. Business flourished as never before. Italy was the center of throbbing commercial activity, and lines of traffic from all parts of the world converged at Rome. Ships in large numbers sailed from port to port in the Mediterranean. Some of the vessels were as much as one hundred eighty feet in length and were capable of carrying as many as six hundred passengers. From the harbor constructed by Claudius at the mouth of the Tiber, a traveler

could board a ship and land in Alexandria in ten days.
A Roman merchant could go by sea to Athens or to Spain
in a week. The network of travel facilities which covered
the Roman world was utilized by the early Christians in
their work of evangelization.

3. *Wide exchange of thought.* The mingling of many
peoples in the Roman Empire made possible an interchange
of ideas on a vast scale. Orientals in large numbers made
their way to the capital. Thousands of Greeks settled in
all the important towns. In every leading city large com-
panies of the Jewish Dispersion established themselves.
Rome itself became the epitome of the world.

Such varied associations contributed to a cosmopolitan
viewpoint. Each person discovered how much he had in
common with his neighbor. Jewish ideas influenced Gentile
thought, and the nationalistic spirit of the Jews was modi-
fied by the more universal outlook of the Greeks and Romans. Narrowness and exclusiveness became less pronounced as men began to think from a more general point
of view. Many of the artisans and traders of the period
were Christians, and while they bought and sold material
things, they also declared the hope of eternal life which is
revealed through Jesus Christ.

4. *Religious tolerance.* Roman polytheism, because of its
indefiniteness, was naturally lenient. The state prescribed
no system of theology. All national cults were allowed
freedom of expression. The Romans incorporated the gods
of conquered peoples into their own pantheon or identified
them with Roman deities. A variety of cults from the East
was popular in the capital and, as long as they were not
considered a threat to the welfare of the community, they
were not restricted. Under Rome's policy of toleration

Christianity was allowed freedom of expression, and it grew unmolested (Acts 28:30-31).

5. *Failure of Roman religion.* The Romans gave their subjects efficient government and military protection, but they could not offer an adequate religion. The Romans were polytheistic and identified their deities with the forces which were thought to control the phenomena of the visible world. Ethical considerations had little place. Religion was looked upon as the observance of certain rituals as a means of securing the aid of the gods. There were large numbers of soothsayers, oracle keepers, and various kinds of priestly functions. Belief in astrology was widespread. Books of magic with formulas for all purposes were circulated.[2]

As the period of the republic drew to a close, religious faith had largely disappeared from the cultivated classes, due in part to the influence of Greek philosophy which questioned the credulity of the time-honored beliefs. During the upheaval of the civil wars there was widespread abandonment of the external ceremonies, and many temples deteriorated.

Augustus attempted to revive the old religion, and he rebuilt many of the temples which lay in ruins in Rome. Nevertheless the days of the early Empire were characterized by religious unrest. Although skepticism and a hopeless fatalism were found among the upper classes, people in general were trying to cling to faith.

The traditional worship had not met the moral and spir-

---

[2]During Paul's ministry at Ephesus, exorcism was exposed and many persons who had been practicing magic made open confession and publicly burned about $10,000.00 worth of their cabalistic formulas (Acts 19:19). This incident illustrates the enormous trade which was carried on in charms. Little scrolls, or pieces of parchment, inscribed with magic words and symbols were worn as amulets.

itual needs of human nature. The prevalence of idolatry
and other primitive religious rites of paganism resulted in
low morality. Prostitution, which was common in the Hellenistic world, was often incorporated into religion. In the
fertility cults, sexual rites were associated with the pro-
ductivity of the fields and of animals and human beings.
The lurid picture of Gentile corruption painted by Paul in
Romans 1:18-32 may be documented from the Greek and
Roman writers of the period. Human behavior was a reflection of the character of the heathen deities. Almost
every imaginable type of licentious conduct was attributed
by the pagans to their gods and goddesses.

It should be noted that the moral degradation of the
Greco-Roman world was not total. Paul implies that there
were some pagans who lived up to the light of conscience
(Rom. 2:14-15). Among the Greeks and Romans there
were thinkers and ethical teachers who sought to de-
fine the good life. Stoicism, the most popular philosophy of the period, with its emphasis upon individual
virtue, seems to have made a notable impression on
the thought of the times. Among the best-known Stoics
were Seneca, Epictetus, and Marcus Aurelius; but of
course there was no redemptive power in their philosoph-
ical system.

Throughout the Roman world multitudes were longing
for assurance about a future life as well as for something
which would give meaning and purpose to their earthly
existence. Large numbers were attracted by the mystery
religions which promised to the initiates salvation and immortality. Cartledge says, "The mysteries especially had
their part to play in preparing the way for the spread of

the Christian gospel. . . . They made men want the things that Christianity could give."[3]

The superiority of Christianity was readily apparent, and in the second century it forged ahead of all other religions of the Empire. In the words of McCasland, "Multitudes of Greeks and Romans heard this good news with joy because in Christ they found the abiding substance for which they had searched their paganism in vain."[4]

THE AUGUSTAN AGE

Prior to the establishment of the Empire, Rome had lacked the impressive array of libraries, theaters, gymnasiums, and other magnificent structures such as those which adorned the principal Hellenistic cities.

Under Augustus and his successors Rome underwent a thorough architectural transformation which made it the foremost art center of the ancient world. Augustus is said to have boasted that he found Rome brick and left it marble. Large public halls for the transaction of business were constructed. A new senate building, planned by Julius Caesar, was built. Caesar had constructed a new forum, but Augustus erected still another, known as the Forum of Augustus, which was placed next to the Forum of Caesar. Augustus built the Temple of the Divine Julius for the worship of his deified foster father. The temple of Minerva, which Pompey had erected in the Campus Martius, Augustus covered with bronze. In honor of his deceased son-in-law, Augustus constructed the Theater of Marcellus. On the Palatine Hill he built of Luna marble a new and lavish temple of Apollo in which were placed splendid works of

---

[3]Samuel A. Cartledge, *A Conservative Introduction to the New Testament*, p. 64.

[4]S. Vernon McCasland, "The Greco-Roman World," *The Interpreter's Bible*, VII, p. 99.

art. The adjoining portico housed libraries of Greek and Latin. Also on the Palatine Augustus built a mansion for his residence. From this *palatium*, or "imperial dwelling," has come the English word "palace," denoting the official residence of a sovereign.

Agrippa, the leading general and minister of Augustus, built the Pantheon in Rome in 27 B.C. As the name implies, the Pantheon was a temple in honor of all the gods. About A.D. 120 Hadrian added the central space or rotunda, which has since formed the main part of the building. The Pantheon, which today remains in an excellent state of preservation, is one of the best examples of ancient Roman architecture.

Augustus gave Rome its first organized police, fire, and water departments, and he set up a definite financial system for the Empire. He wanted to know the amount of finances needed to carry on the government, and how much of this amount each province should justly contribute in the form of taxes. To answer these questions he ordered thorough census lists and property assessments. The Gospel of Luke mentions the first decree of registration issued by Augustus (Luke 2:1-5). Much of the tax money was returned to the provinces to pay for public works and buildings.

Although architecture flourished in the Augustan Age, there was a lack of science. Rome had produced no individuals comparable to Archimedes, the Greek mathematician, and Eratosthenes, the Greek geographer of the third century B.C, men of the illustrious line of scientists whose achievements made the Hellenistic Age the greatest period of science in the pre-Christian era. The best geography of the Augustan Age was prepared by Strabo (63? B.C.–A.D.

24?), a Greek geographer and historian who lived in Rome. Strabo's work was lacking in scientific method, but for several centuries his volumes were the world's standard books in the field.

Despite the lack of science in the Augustan Age, there was much interest in literature. The most prominent Romans of the late Republic, Julius Caesar (100-44 B.C.) and Cicero (106-43 B.C.), were men of the utmost ability in public leadership and in literary accomplishment. Men of their class were well versed in the best works of Greek thought. Even while Caesar was encumbered with the heavy responsibilities of his wars in Gaul, he wrote a treatise on Latin speech. Cicero was the supreme master of Latin prose, and the foremost orator in Roman history. Breasted calls Cicero "the most cultivated man Rome ever produced," and he says that "the ideals of the educated man which he himself personified have never ceased to exert a powerful influence upon educated men in all lands."[5] The merging of Greek and Roman civilization, which was expressed in Ciceronian culture, was the inspiration of the Augustan Age.

The leading Latin poets were Horace (65-8 B.C.) and Vergil (70-19 B.C.). Their works are a reflection of the men, customs, and ideas of Augustan society. They wrote mainly for court circles and the upper middle class, whose favor was necessary for the preservation of the constitution. Thus Horace and Vergil were important political assets in their day. However, their lasting influence has been rendered to universal literature.

Horace had studied in Athens and was acquainted with

---

[5]James Henry Breasted, *Ancient Times: A History of the Early World,* p. 614.

the old Greek lyric poets. Literary students have been attracted to him not only by the form and substance of his writings, but by the frankness of his self-revelation. Breasted says the poems of Horace are "a treasury of Roman life as pictured by a ripe and cultivated mind. . . ."[6]

Vergil's *Aeneid* is one of the masterpieces of world literature. It is in twelve books and is patterned after Homer's *Iliad* and *Odyssey*. It was composed to glorify the city of Rome and the ancestors of Julius and Augustus Caesar. Such a theme lent itself to legendary and mythological elements. As the national epic of Rome, the *Aeneid* tells of the adventures of the Trojan hero, Aeneas, who led a band of followers from Asia Minor to found a new nation in Italy. Aeneas is regarded as the forefather of the royal line of the Caesars. Vergil prepared his epic at the request of Augustus, who was his personal friend. Vergil was a meticulous workman. He gave many years in preparation for the task, and he spent eleven years on the first draft of the poem. At the time of his death he was still revising his production which he felt had fallen short of his exalted standard of achievement.

In an age acquainted with the literary ability of Julius Caesar, with the oratory of Cicero, and with the poetic skill of Horace and Vergil, Paul wrote his Epistle to the Romans. Seen in the perspective of the centuries and appraised from the standpoint of its depth of insight and abiding relevance, Paul's treatise is an incomparable classic. Its supreme excellence lies in the fact that it is a masterly exposition of the changeless love which God has revealed in Jesus the Christ for the salvation of every human being who will trust in Him.

---

[6]*Ibid.*, p. 615.

CHAPTER II

The Church at Rome

It is not known exactly when or how the gospel first reached Rome, but it may be regarded as certain that Christianity was introduced in the capital of the Empire soon after Pentecost.

EARLY ESTABLISHMENT

The church at Rome had a relatively long history when Paul wrote to it. By that time it was on a firm basis and was well known as an influential congregation (Rom. 1:8; 16:19).

We have no direct evidence concerning the founding of the church at Rome. The Epistle reveals nothing which gives a positive answer to this question. The supposition that the Apostle Peter established the congregation has no scriptural support. The Petrine tradition can be traced no earlier than the latter part of the second century. Irenaeus (*Against Heresies*, III. 3),[1] who wrote about A.D. 185 (and he seems to have been the first to make the claim) states that the church at Rome was founded by Peter and Paul. The church historian Eusebius,[2] writing more than a hundred years later, says that it was founded by Peter. Perhaps disciples won to Christ by Peter and Paul (and by others) were instrumental in starting the church in Rome.

---

[1]Cf. *The Ante-Nicene Fathers,* Vol. I, p. 415. The statement contains at least one error, for the Epistle to the Romans makes it clear that Paul was not a founder of the church at Rome. Such an error casts doubt upon the historical trustworthiness of the assertion. However, it is significant that the tradition which it reflects has no thought of the primacy of Peter.

[2]Cf. Kirsopp Lake (trans.), *Eusebius: The Ecclesiastical History* (Loeb Classical Library), I, 141-143.

It may have been because of this that Peter and Paul were mentioned as instrumental in helping to found it. Eusebius, desiring to connect Peter with Rome, leaves out the name of Paul and gives Peter the credit of being the founder.

Acts supports the view of the early establishment of the church at Rome. Priscilla and Aquila seem to have been Christians in Rome (Acts 18:2) when the Claudian edict expelled the Jews (Claudius was Emperor of Rome A.D. 41-54). It may have been because the Christians had greatly increased in the Roman capital, and had thereby occasioned hostile movements by the Jews against them, that Claudius issued the edict.

According to Acts 15, Peter was still in Palestine many years after the establishment of the church in Rome. He was present in Jerusalem at the apostolic conference (Acts 15:7; cf. Gal. 2:9) about A.D. 49; hence it is reasonable to assume that he did not visit Rome until years after the church there was established, if he went there at all.

At the Jerusalem conference, on the basis of the work being carried on by Peter and Paul (Gal. 2:8), it was recognized that Paul had been entrusted with the gospel for the uncircumcised (the Gentiles), and that Peter had been entrusted with the gospel for the circumcision (the Jews, vs. 7). Such recognition militates against the idea that Peter had been engaged in preaching west of the territory in which Paul had been working.

The Epistle to the Romans implies that Peter had not been in Rome when the letter was written. In the sixteenth chapter[3] of Romans Paul names more than a score of friends he had in the church at Rome, but Peter's name

---

[3]Although some interpreters think Romans 16 was originally written to Ephesus, other scholars hold that the list of names in that chapter is compatible with the Roman destination.

is missing. Would Paul fail to mention Peter if the latter had ever been in Rome and had a part in establishing the church? Paul was too tactful for that! Knox says, "Paul would almost certainly have made some reference to Peter's connection with the church at Rome if any such connection had existed."[4]

When Paul finally reached Rome, three years after sending the Epistle, Peter had not yet been there (cf. Acts 28). When Paul wrote to the Philippians, near the end of his first Roman imprisonment, there is still no evidence that Peter had visited Rome. This indicates that as late as the early sixties Peter had not arrived in the imperial capital.

It is possible that Peter may have been in Rome during the Neronian persecution.[5] The best scriptural argument in this regard is First Peter 5:13, if Babylon means Rome, as it does in the Apocalypse of John. Mark is with Peter, and it is clear that Mark was with Paul in Rome earlier (Col. 4:10).

Both Peter and Paul may have been martyred at Rome, as tradition states,[6] but there is no ground for supposing that Peter established the church there. Goodspeed says of the church at Rome, "The legend connecting Peter with its foundation is clearly unhistorical."[7]

THEORIES OF FOUNDING

There are several plausible theories regarding the beginning of the church at Rome. We mention the following possibilities:

---

[4]John Knox and Gerald R. Cragg, *The Epistle to the Romans* (The Interpreter's Bible, Vol. IX), p. 362.

[5]Cf. Lake, *op. cit.*, p. 181.

[6]*Loc. cit.* Oscar Cullman (*Peter: Disciple–Apostle–Martyr,* trans. by Floyd V. Filson) discusses literary, liturgical, and archaeological data bearing upon the question of Peter's residence in Rome.

[7]Edgar J. Goodspeed, *An Introduction to the New Testament,* p. 70.

1. It could have been established by Roman Jews and proselytes from Pentecost. On that notable occasion, when the disciples received the Holy Spirit, people from Rome were present in Jerusalem (Acts 2:10). Some of them may have been converted and carried back to Rome an account of the wonders witnessed on that day.

2. Christianity in Rome may have originated through the synagogues. There were thousands of Jews in Rome, and they were in constant touch with Jerusalem. Christian Jews could have communicated the message of Jesus to friends in the world metropolis. In the synagogues were proselytes whose attachment to Judaism was not rigid, and whose receptivity to the gospel would have been greater than that of persons who were Jews by birth.

3. The church may have been founded by Hellenists who fled to Rome during the persecution following the death of Stephen.

4. Some members of the Italian cohort may have followed the example of Cornelius (Acts 10:1) in embracing the Christian faith, and thereafter planted the gospel in Rome.

5. A converging of Christian travelers from various places could have led to the founding of the church at Rome. People from all over the Empire were naturally attracted to the capital. Early Christianity was spread by many lay witnesses wherever they went. Some obscure believers, going about in the course of their ordinary business, may have journeyed to Rome and become the nucleus of the congregation there.

6. The church might possibly have been established by converts of Paul. The Apostle preached in all the chief cities east of Italy and won many converts. No doubt a

number of them went to Rome. However, the Epistle gives no indication that the congregation at Rome was indebted to Paul as its founder.

COMPOSITION

Dibelius[8] sees reflected in Romans "nothing of the to and fro of a genuine correspondence," and he thinks it is useless to look for an answer in the Epistle to the much discussed question of the composition of the church at Rome. He points out that it is a difficult problem inasmuch as the character of the congregation was continually changing.

If the church was established by Jewish Christians, probably in the beginning the converts were mostly Jewish. However, soon afterwards and especially when Paul wrote, it appears that the congregation was composed largely of Gentiles.

Paul writes as though both Jewish and Gentile Christians were in the church at Rome. A number of passages indicate the presence of Jewish Christians. Paul addresses Jews directly at times (cf. 2:17, 27). Much of the argument of the Epistle is addressed to persons of Jewish background. Paul reasons with Jews who would justify themselves (2:17—3:9). He calls Abraham "our natural forefather" (4:1). He answers objections to his doctrine of freedom from the Law (6:1—7:6). His treatment of the Mosaic Code and the principle of justification (chapters 4—7) were of highest importance to Jews. His philosophy of history concerns the obduracy of Israel (chapters 9—11). Those persons who made distinctions between various foods

---

[8]Martin Dibelius, *A Fresh Approach to the New Testament and Early Christian Literature,* p. 162.

(14:2-3) and between different days (14:5-6) were probably Jews. The basic aim of the entire Epistle is to show that righteousness is the result of justification by faith apart from the works of law. Thus it is a detailed statement of the supremacy of faith, and a vindication of Paul's gospel. All this implies an audience of Jewish background.

On the other hand, many passages indicate the presence of a Gentile constituency in the church at Rome. Paul's ground for writing is the fact that he is the apostle of the Gentiles, and he explicitly addresses the Romans as Gentiles (1:5-7, 13-15; 11:13, 25, 28, 30). He finds authority for his vigorous language because he is the minister of Jesus Christ among the Gentiles (15:15-16). He desires to visit the Roman believers in order that he might gather some fruit among them as among other Gentiles (1:13-14). Paul's argument in 11:17-32 presupposes a great many Gentiles, with whom the Jews are contrasted. The "strong" believers of chapters 14 and 15 probably were Gentile Christians who were not so scrupulous regarding matters of conscience as were the Jewish Christians.

According to Denney,[9] Beyschlag suggests that the church consisted mainly of proselytes, which would explain why Paul addresses the readers as if they were Gentiles but reasons with them as if they were Jews.

It seems safe to conclude, with the prevailing view of present-day exegetes, that the majority of the church at Rome were Gentile Christians. The salutations at the end of the Epistle lend force to this conclusion, for although some of the names are Jewish, most of them are Gentile and mainly Greek.

The matter of chief importance is the doctrinal position

---

[9]James Denney, *St. Paul's Epistle to the Romans* (The Expositor's Greek Testament, Vol. II), p. 561.

of the Roman believers. Did the Jewish Christian viewpoint prevail, or was a more liberal outlook dominant?
Were the relations between the Jewish and the Gentile
members of the church cordial, or had problems developed
to the extent that normal progress was retarded?

We may suppose that the Jewish Christians in Rome, as
elsewhere, retained to a more or less extent their regard
for the Mosaic Law. It was likely, and the Epistle reflects
the idea, that some of them maintained their traditional
attitude in observing some of the Mosaic rituals and in
abstaining from certain meats. But it appears that the
majority of the church was free from Jewish scruples. Dods
observes, "Had the Church been to any large extent tainted
with distinctively Jewish-Christian views, Paul could not
have spoken of its members as 'full of all goodness, filled
with all knowledge, able also to admonish one another'
(Rom. xv. 14)."[10]

The church seems to have had no internal disturbances[11]
beyond differences of opinion indicated by the two groups
which Paul designates the "weak" and the "strong" (14:1-2;
15:1).

The expression *tēi pistei, the faith* (14:1) appears to
indicate not so much faith in the subjective sense of personal trust as it does faith in the objective sense of Christian
doctrine, although both meanings are involved in the idea.
Specifically, in this context, the faith seems to denote the
apprehension of the Christian viewpoint regarding food,

---

[10]Marcus Dods, *An Introduction to the New Testament,* p. 91.
[11]R. C. H. Lenski (*The Interpretation of St. Paul's Epistle to the Romans,*
p. 915) notes the present infinitive *skopein* in Romans 16:17, "*be keeping
your eyes open for*" division makers, and he thinks such errorists were not
yet present in Rome, but that Paul warns the church to be on guard in
case they appear. Cf. Sanday and Headlam, *The Epistle to the Romans* (The
International Critical Commentary), p. 429.

observance of certain days, and the like. Persons are "weak" in the faith who are not able to distinguish between essentials and nonessentials. Denney interprets the faith here as "saving reliance on Christ," but he adds, "and all that it involves." He says, "One is weak in respect of faith who does not understand that salvation is of faith from first to last, and that faith is secured by its own entireness and intensity, not by timorous scrupulosity of conscience."[12]

Were the "weak" for whom Paul urges tolerance Jewish or Gentile Christians? Probably they were the former, but not necessarily so. They may have been Gentile Christians affected by neo-Pythagorean philosophy, the asceticism of which was similar to the Essenic. According to Barmby,[13] this is the view of Eichhorn. But Barmby thinks Jewish influences are much more probable, and he notes that Origen makes a clear distinction between Christian and Pythagorean asceticism. Denney[14] observes that although the "weak" need not have been Jews, their scruples had Jewish affinities.

---

[12]Denney, *op. cit.*, p. 701.
[13]J. Barmby, *The Epistle of Paul to the Romans* (The Pulpit Commentary, Vol. 18), p. 409.
[14]Denney, *loc. cit.*

CHAPTER III

The Epistle to the Romans

That Paul is the author of Romans has been and remains the position of New Testament scholars generally. The traditional view is based upon commanding external and internal evidence.

Acquaintance with Romans is reflected in several other New Testament books, including First and Second Peter, the Fourth Gospel, and Hebrews. The Apostolic Fathers[1], e.g. Clement of Rome (A.D. 95), Ignatius of Antioch (ca. 98-110), and Polycarp, Bishop of Smyrna (in the first half of the second century), display the knowledge and influence of Romans. In the Muratorian Canon (ca. 170-200), Romans stands ninth in the list of Paul's letters. Knox says, "Every list or canon of the Pauline letters of which we have any knowledge—orthodox or heretical—has contained it [Romans]."[2] Thiessen observes, "From Irenaeus onward the references to Romans are full and complete in all the Church writers; it is uniformly recognized as by Paul and as canonical."[3]

The Epistle itself names Paul as the author (1:1). The vocabulary, literary style, and doctrinal character are Pauline. The background reflected in the letter fits in with the career of Paul as we know it from his other acknowledged writings and from Acts. Knox states, "Few facts can be surer than that the letter, at least in major part, is from

---

[1]Cf. Kirsopp Lake (trans.), *The Apostolic Fathers* (Loeb Classical Library), Vol. I.
[2]John Knox and Gerald R. Cragg, *op. cit.*, p. 356.
[3]Henry Clarence Thiessen, *Introduction to the New Testament*, p. 220.

Paul's hand. The evidences of authenticity are so impressive, severally and cumulatively, as to make the case altogether irrefutable."[4]

Relatively early in Christian history Romans was placed first in the list of Paul's letters,[5] and it maintains this distinction in our New Testaments although in the actual chronology of the Apostle's correspondence several other epistles were written first.

PREEMINENT TREATISE

In logical arrangement and in detailed doctrinal elucidation Romans is the most impressive of the New Testament epistles. It has many characteristics of a letter in the usual sense, especially the personal elements in the beginning and near the close, but it is more than a letter. It is so profound in content and so systematic in presentation that it may be classified as a theological treatise. It deals in an appealing manner with general issues, and contains little of the polemic tone which is so prominent in the Corinthian and Galatian correspondence. Taylor notes in Romans the interblending of "argument and experience, instruction and exhortation, doxology and benediction."[6] Denney[7] calls Romans a work of vitality, comprehensive scope, infinite variety of application, and a writing which is personal and historical, universal and eternal. Goodspeed views the Epistle as "positively awe-inspiring," and he says, "No book

[4]Knox and Cragg, *op. cit.*, p. 355.

[5]Albert E. Barnett (*The New Testament, Its Making and Meaning*, p. 59) says, "From the fourth century onward, Romans regularly stands at the head of the list of Paul's letters in the Greek manuscripts and in the manuscripts of the versions." For historic lists of the New Testament books, see Edgar J. Goodspeed, *The Formation of the New Testament*, pp. 187-203.

[6]William M. Taylor, *Paul the Missionary*, p. 348.

[7]Denney, *op. cit.*, p. 568.

of the New Testament appears more formidable to the modern reader than Romans."[8]

In contrast to Paul's other epistles, most of which were written in the heat of theological conflict, Romans was composed under conditions of comparative leisure. The Epistle makes little reference to actual circumstances within the congregation, except in chapters fourteen and fifteen where the "strong" and the "weak" are directed to exercise forbearance toward each other. Dibelius remarks, "Among the Pauline letters Romans is the least conditioned by the momentary situation . . ."[9]

With but brief if any negative argument Romans is a positive presentation of the cardinal doctrines of the Christian message. Inasmuch as the development of Paul's theme is not disturbed by torrid pastoral problems, Romans, more than any other of the Apostle's writings, reveals his method of presenting the gospel. In his other letters theological reflection comes in more or less incidentally, but in Romans Paul directly and extensively sets forth his doctrinal convictions, especially the relation between faith and works, and defends them by logical discussion. In the words of Hunter, "Surely it is that in Romans we have the answer to the question, 'What is Christianity?' by the strongest thinker in the early Church."[10]

Romans is of course an ancient masterpiece of religious literature, but it is more than an admirable work of the past. It has timeless relevance because it deals with questions which recur in every generation. The problems of men individually and collectively are essentially the same in each period of history. Romans answers the vital queries

[8]Goodspeed, *op. cit.*, p. 73.
[9]Dibelius, *op. cit.*, p. 161.
[10]Hunter, *op. cit.*, p. 96.

of anthropology, hamartiology, and soteriology. In no other writing do we have such a penetrating analysis of human personality and such a glorious answer to the human quest. The Socratic maxim, "Know thyself," finds its fulfillment in the insights made known in the letter to the Romans. The majestic scope of Paul's vision extends from his glimpse of the divine purpose which antedates time to its consummation beyond history, when we shall realize our ultimate destiny through Jesus Christ our Lord (Rom. 8:28-39).

OCCASION AND PURPOSE

For a number of years Paul had been eager to visit the church at Rome, but his responsibilities had kept him in the East (1:10-13; 15:23). After his fruitful ministry at Ephesus, with its outreach into the surrounding territories (Acts 19), Paul felt that his labors in Asia Minor and the Grecian peninsula were almost at an end (Rom. 15:23). Other evangelists were preaching in Syria, Egypt, the northern part of Asia Minor, and in Italy. What should he do now?

Paul's principle of operation was to work in regions where the gospel had not been proclaimed (Rom. 15:20; 2 Cor. 10:16). He was a planter; others could water. That is, he laid the foundations; others could erect the superstructures (1 Cor. 3:6, 10). Although for an extended period certain exigencies pressed Paul into pastoral care, as Galatians and First and Second Corinthians reveal (cf. Acts 15:36, 41; 18:23), the untouched fields were constantly upon his heart.

Now Paul's thoughts turned to Spain. There an open field awaited him. Roman roadways had stimulated travel and communication and had linked Spain with the new world. Materially and culturally Spain was experiencing an awakening and Paul saw it as an inviting mission field. So he began to plan a journey to the far West, expecting to plant the gospel in the Roman provinces there (Rom. 15:24, 28). But Paul knew that he must have a springboard of operation if he were to work effectively in the new project. Rome would be the logical center from which to launch the venture, just as Syrian Antioch had been an effective base for campaigns in the East (Acts 11:26; 13:1-3; 15:36-41; 18:22-23).

Paul wanted to be assured of the sympathy and cooperation of the congregation at Rome. He knew how important the influential capital would be as a center for the promotion of the missionary enterprise. He decided to communicate with the Roman Christians, lay his plan before them, and ask for their support. Their good will would be very helpful, as well as their temporal aid. If they understood Paul's mission and were his friends, they could protect him against insidious attacks by his enemies. Jewish reactionaries had opposed Paul in Galatia and Corinth. If such antagonists were to circulate false rumors about him in the capital, the church could be prejudiced against him and that would be a hindrance to his work.

The object of the Epistle is thus clearly indicated. Paul writes for the purpose of preparing the church at Rome for his visit, and in the hope of securing support for his endeavor in the West. He is anxious to proclaim in the mightiest city of the world the glorious message which is capable of meeting all the needs of the human heart. But, in accord with his principle of not working in areas already evangelized, Paul intended to preach in Rome only while journeying through (Rom. 15:24).

Along with the announcement of his prospective visit, Paul takes advantage of the correspondence to give the Romans a thorough statement of his gospel. When they have a clear understanding of his viewpoint, they will be the more disposed to cooperate wholeheartedly with him. While enjoying a period of relative leisure, Paul had time to formulate more fully than previously a general expression of his theology. Therefore, in this Epistle we have a comprehensive discussion of the character of the righteousness made known in Jesus Christ.

Paul anticipated his journey to Rome, and to the regions beyond, "in the fullness of Christ's blessing" (Rom. 15:29). He looked forward to the privilege of imparting some spiritual benefit to the Roman brethren, and to receiving encouragement from their faith (1:11-12).

DATE AND PLACE OF WRITING

The place and the approximate time in which Romans was composed are not difficult to ascertain. From the account of Paul's movements which we gather from Acts and from several of his letters, we are able to put together the setting out of which Paul wrote the Epistle to the Romans.

Soon after the riot in the theater at Ephesus (Acts 19:29), Paul left that city in accordance with his purpose (vs. 21), and proceeded toward Macedonia (20:1). Prior to departing from Ephesus, he had sent Titus to Corinth to deal with pressing problems in the congregation there. Paul expected to meet Titus at Troas and to hear the report of his mission.

When Paul reached Troas, Titus did not meet him there. This caused Paul to fear that matters had deteriorated at Corinth. At that time there was a challenging opportunity for the gospel in the vicinity of Troas, but Paul was to apprehensive about the Corinthians to take advantage of it, so he hurried on into Macedonia (2 Cor. 2:12-13).

At length Titus met Paul at an unnamed point in Macedonia, likely at Philippi where Paul had a number of friends, and gave him a report which was very encouraging (2 Cor. 7:5-7). The Corinthians had honored Paul's appeal and had assumed their responsibility in dealing with the case of incest (2:5-11; cf. 1 Cor. 5). But there were still difficulties with a restive minority which questioned Paul's apostolic authority (cf. 2 Cor. 10-13).

Paul wrote Second Corinthians, probably from Philippi, and sent Titus back to Corinth with the letter, trusting that his faithful lieutenant could clear up the problems. Paul remained in Macedonia for a time, hoping that during the interval the Corinthians would profit by his written exhortations (2 Cor. 13).

Luke does not tell us how long Paul remained in Macedonia at this time, but it seems to have been a considerable period, for Paul went through those parts of Macedonia where he had founded churches (i.e., Philippi, Thessalonica, and Berea) and exhorted them with much speech (Acts 20:2). It must have been also during this period that Paul extended his sphere of operations as far as Illyricum (Rom. 15:19).[11]

Bruce[12] estimates that something over a year was required for Paul's activities from the time he left Ephesus,

---

[11]Illyricum, known also as Dalmatia (2 Tim. 4:10) was a province of the Roman Empire located on the Adriatic Sea above the west coast of Macedonia. Paul's journey to the Illyrian border is assigned to the period of his second visit to Macedonia. His first Macedonian visit, the movements of which are fully recorded (Acts 16:12–17:15), did not bring him near the Illyrian frontier.

[12]F. F. Bruce, *The Book of Acts* (The New International Commentary on the New Testament), p. 405.

including his stay at Troas and his ministry in Macedonia, until his arrival in Greece, and he dates the period from the summer of A.D. 55 to the late part of A.D. 56.

We know from Acts 20:2-6 that Paul spent the next three months in Greece, and that he left Greece shortly before Easter, celebrated Easter at Philippi, and then proceeded toward Jerusalem. Going back a little, we gather from First Corinthians 16:6 that Paul had planned to spend the winter at Corinth. (In Second Corinthians 13:1 he tells of his forthcoming visit; and according to Acts 20:3 he originally intended to sail from Greece to Syria). So we may conclude that Paul remained the greater part of the three months in Corinth. These were the winter months of A.D. 56-57, probably, and Paul was a guest in the home of his friend Gaius (Rom. 16:23). This disciple seems identical with the Corinthian whom Paul personally baptized (1 Cor. 1:14).

During this three months' stay in Corinth, Paul found time to compose the Epistle to the Romans. Phoebe, a servant or deacon[13] of the church at Cenchreae, the eastern port of Corinth, is commended (Rom. 16:1) to the church at Rome,[14] and she may have been the bearer of the Epistle.

The one duty which remained for Paul to discharge, as he concluded his work in the eastern world, was to deliver the funds contributed by the Gentile churches of the Roman provinces of Galatia, Asia, Macedonia, and Achaia for the

---

[13]The Greek term *diakonos* is common gender.
[14]It is here assumed that Romans 16 was an original part of the Epistle.

relief of the needy saints in Palestine (Rom. 15:25-28; 2 Cor. 8—9). The collections were to be handled by delegates representing the participating congregations (1 Cor. 16:1-4; Acts 20:4), who arranged to make the voyage with Paul and present the money to the elders at Jerusalem.[15]

It was Paul's intention to sail directly from Corinth to the East, but upon learning that Jewish enemies were plotting to kill him, he eluded them by going through Macedonia (Acts 20:3). Romans makes no mention of this change of plan, and thus implies that the Epistle was written and sent before the discovery of the plot, i.e. before Paul's departure from Corinth.

The date of Romans, therefore, is definitely towards the end of Paul's second visit to the Grecian peninsula. The Epistle was written in the spring, for when Paul was about to leave Corinth navigation was possible, although he was compelled to take the land route through Macedonia. He reached Macedonia before the Passover (Acts 20:6), and he expected to arrive at Jerusalem before the Day of Pentecost (20:16). The precise year in which Romans was composed depends upon one's view of Pauline chronology, but most interpreters fix the date as ± A.D. 57. It is clear that Romans was written after the Corinthian correspondence, and probably also after the Epistle to the Galatians.

---

[15]This offering was not only to alleviate the physical needs of the saints in Jerusalem, but also Paul hoped it would serve to convince the Jewish Christians of their common bond with the Gentile Christians. One of Paul's most frequent points of emphasis in his letters was the unity of all believers in Christ (Rom. 12:5; 1 Cor. 10:17; 12:12f.; Gal. 3:28f.; Eph. 2:13-22).

CHAPTER IV

Integrity and Contents of Romans

FORM OF THE EPISTLE

A number of modern scholars hold that the sixteenth chapter of Romans did not belong originally to the Epistle. They favor the hypothesis of David Schulz (1829) who suggested that the chapter was a fragment of a letter first sent elsewhere, probably to Ephesus, and later attached to Romans. This opinion is based upon such textual data as the following:

1. The numerous salutations (16:3-15). It is thought unlikely that Paul could have known so many people in a church which as yet he had not visited. On the other hand, the Apostle had lived and worked in Ephesus for more than two years and knew many persons there. Hence an Ephesian destination is presumed to be more compatible with the list of names.

2. A seeming plurality of terminations. Romans appears to contain several endings (15:13, 33; 16:20, 27). It is supposed that these expressions, which are taken as final, indicate compilation, possibly by extractions from other correspondence.

3. The doxology (16:25-27) is found in different places in the extant Greek manuscripts. In many cursives and in one or two uncials the doxology stands at the end of chapter fourteen. Some manuscripts contain it in both chapters, and a few omit it entirely. The Chester Beatty Papyrus (P[46]), which gives us a text from about the middle of the

45

third century, has the doxology at the end of chapter fifteen. From these phenomena it has been inferred that chapter sixteen was not an integral part of Romans.

Although the foregoing suppositions have some appeal, they are not conclusive. Other considerations, equally if not more weighty, militate against them:

1. It is highly probable that Paul had a sizable circle of acquaintances in Rome. His missionary activities had brought him into contact with individuals in all the principal towns of the East. Travel between Rome and the Orient was common, facilitated by the excellent Roman roads and by the numerous ships plying the Mediterranean. Therefore many of Paul's friends may have settled in Rome and become part of the local church. The Apostle would inevitably remember them as he concluded his letter and, in anticipation of his visit, would extend greetings to them.

Questions have been raised about the presence of Aquila and Priscilla, who are greeted in Romans 16:3. Although these friends were residents of Ephesus when Paul wrote First Corinthians (1 Cor. 16:19), and were in Ephesus when the Pastoral Epistles were written (2 Tim. 4:19), it is not improbable that they were in Rome when Paul addressed the church there. The course of events necessitated considerable traveling on the part of Aquila and Priscilla. When they were banished from Rome by the edict of Claudius, they came to Corinth. There they met Paul and gave him employment in their establishment (Acts 18:2-3). Later they resided in Ephesus (vss. 18-19, 26) and, when no longer prevented by the Claudian decree[1] they, as did many other Jews and Jewish Christians, may well have returned to Rome where they were included

---

[1]Apparently the expulsion commanded by Claudius was conditional and only temporary. Cf. J. B. Lightfoot, *Biblical Essays*, p. 301.

in Paul's greeting. Several years afterward, during the Apostle's final Roman imprisonment, they were again in Ephesus. This amount of travel for Aquila and Priscilla will not be considered unusual when it is remembered that they were itinerant Jewish artisans and merchants. Lightfoot says of this couple's nomadic life:

They were wanderers not only by the exigencies of their trade, but also by the obligations of their missionary work. Why should we deny them a rapidity of movement, which we are obliged to concede to Timotheus, to Tychicus, to St. Luke, to St. Paul himself?[2]

Regarding the list of names in Romans 16, Denney writes:

It is, as Gifford points out, a very strong, indeed a conclusive argument for the Roman destination of the letter, that of the twenty-two persons named in verses 6-15, not one can be shown to have been at Ephesus; while (1) Urbanus, Rufus, Ampliatus, Julia and Junia are specifically Roman names, and (2) besides the first four of these names, "ten others, Stachys, Apelles, Tryphaena, Tryphosa, Hermes, Hermas, Patrobas (or Patrobius), Philologus, Julia, Nereus are found in the sepulchral inscriptions on the Appian Way as the names of persons connected with 'Caesar's household' (Phil. iv. 22), and contemporary with St. Paul."[3]

2. The passages classified by some interpreters as terminal are probably postscripts. Paul often added to his epistles statements in his own handwriting. His postscripts at times included hortatory elements (1 Cor. 16:21-24; Gal. 6:11-18). Romans 16:21-24 is clearly a postscript. Paul may have intended to give the doxology immediately following his prayer of verse 20, and thus close the Epistle. But at that point it must have occurred to him to send the salutations of his associates, some of whom (16:21) had no doubt just arrived in Corinth from Macedonia with the col-

---

[2]*Loc. cit.*
[3]Denney, *op. cit.*, p. 581.

lections for the saints in Jerusalem. Consequently Paul inserted the greetings following the prayer, after which he terminated the Epistle with the doxology.

3. In some of the foremost manuscripts, including Codex Vaticanus, Codex Sinaiticus, and other uncials, the doxology appears only at 16:25-27. In the Syriac, Vulgate, and other early versions, and in the Latin Fathers, the doxology stands consistently at the end of the sixteenth chapter.

The doxology is exceedingly appropriate as the conclusion of Romans. It seems even more fitting for Paul to have closed with a doxology than with a benediction (e.g. 15:33; 16:20). His ascription of praise is majestic in thought and form and is in keeping with the character of the Epistle. It has a distinct relevance to the content and tone of the entire document, and it emphasizes the revelation upon which the message of the Epistle is based.

Why is the doxology found at the end of chapter fourteen in some of the later readings? Lectionaries were probably responsible for its insertion there. From such an arbitrary arrangement the doxology could have found its way easily into the fourteenth chapter of the later manuscripts and versions. Denney says:

> Possibly the lectionaries explain its appearance at this point. The matter in chaps. xv. and xvi. being of a more personal or temporary interest was not likely to be chosen for reading in church. But in order that the great doxology, which was too short for a lesson by itself, might not be lost in public worship, it was appended to the last lesson before chap. xv.[4]

Many scholars, including Hort,[5] Moule,[6] Sanday and

---

[4]Denney, *op. cit.*, p. 576.
[5]Lightfoot, *op. cit.*, pp. 321-351.
[6]Handley C. G. Moule, *The Epistle to the Romans*, p. vi.

Headlam,[7] Robertson,[8] Stifler,[9] and Lenski[10] hold that chapter sixteen was addressed originally to Rome and that it was contemporaneous with the rest of the letter. The present writer sees no formidable reason for doubting that the Epistle to the Romans, as we have it, is both authentic and integral.

ANALYSIS

The Epistle to the Romans is an exposition of the character of true righteousness—the righteousness which is conditioned on faith. In no other extant writing of Paul is the essential nature of Christianity so fully and formally stated.

After his opening remarks to the church at Rome, Paul introduces the central theme of the Epistle, which is *dikaiosunē theou,* meaning "God's kind[11] of righteousness" (1:17). This is the recurring thesis of the composition (cf. 3:5, 21-22), and the entire theological argument of the letter reflects the implications of this major concept.

In the context of Romans, "God's kind of righteousness" does not mean the moral rectitude which inheres in the Supreme Being, but it signifies man's awareness of having been brought into right relationship with God. It denotes the acquittal from guilt which God pronounces upon every individual who places trust in his Son. It is through the gospel of Jesus Christ that the righteousness which is of divine quality is made effective; hence Paul calls the message "the power of God unto salvation" (1:16). The potency

---

[7]Sanday and Headlam, *op. cit.*, pp. lxxxv-xcviii.

[8]Archibald Thomas Robertson, *Word Pictures in the New Testament,* Vol. IV, pp. 320-321.

[9]James M. Stifler, *The Epistle to the Romans,* pp. 13-15.

[10]Lenski, *op. cit.*, pp. 6, 20.

[11]Indicated by the anarthrous construction. The nonuse of the article with the noun in the genitive lays stress upon the qualitative force of the noun.

of the gospel resides not alone in the ethical truths disclosed therein, but in the *dunamis,* or dynamic energy, of God which is exerted personally by the Holy Spirit in everyone who believes. Every aspect of salvation, from the beginning throughout, is based upon faith (1:17).

Paul begins the treatment of his theme by pointing out the world's need of righteousness (1:18—3:20). The need is apparent from the obvious results of wickedness. The indictment is comprehensive. Morally, all men are in the same category (3:22). Jews as well as Gentiles are under condemnation. All need salvation because all have sinned, and the race continues to fall short of God's standard (vs. 23).

The Gentiles had been given some knowledge of God through the witness of the created universe, but instead of retaining this awareness they worshiped the works of their own hands (1:18-23). Idolatry expressed itself in debasing religion and vile conduct. Consequently God gave them over to punishment (vss. 24-32).

The fact that the Jews were given a written revelation will not save them because they have not lived up to the requirements of the Law. Furthermore it is impossible to keep the Law perfectly. The Jews who, in their spiritual pride, condemned the Gentiles, could not escape God's judgment, for the Jews themselves practiced the very things which they condemned in others (2:1-24). Paul overthrows the pretensions of the Jews by proving from their own Scriptures that "there is not a righteous person, not even one!" (3:10). Inasmuch as none could perfectly observe the whole Law, righteousness by works was impossible.

Actually the Law was not intended to save men; it was given to reveal sin (3:20). The Law was powerless to achieve righteousness in man owing to the weakness of human nature, the sphere in which the Law had to operate (8:3). Man's depraved nature, the sinful tendency inherited from Adam (5:12; 7:12-23), had set him at enmity against God (8:7). The legislation by which the Jew hoped to be saved had brought only the realization of sin, and the Law's commandments had actually served as an incitement to transgression (7:8-11). Thus the impotency of the Mosaic Code had left the Jew in a miserable state (vs. 24).

But for the Gentile and the Jewish world, alike under guilt and condemnation, Paul has good news: God himself has provided the salvation which men could never achieve. God has demonstrated his own saving righteousness by a glorious act of redemption in Jesus Christ (3:24-26). Thus the Law, which no man could fulfill, is satisfied and the righteousness based on faith becomes the possession of the believer. Paul emphasizes the fact that salvation is offered as God's free gift, apart from law. It comes through faith —a sense of personal trust in Jesus. Faith is the one condition of salvation for all persons, whether Jews or Gentiles. Because it is a matter of faith, the gospel recognizes no social or national distinctions (3:22-23). Paul calls upon Jews and Gentiles to lay aside boasting and, on an equal footing, to receive justification by faith in Jesus Christ (vss. 27-30).

Paul goes on to show that justification by faith is no new doctrine. In God's redemptive plan faith has always been the indispensable factor. This is illustrated in the history of Abraham who, long before the Mosaic Law was given, was accepted by God on the basis of faith (4:1-22). Abraham did not merit God's favor by his works. He was justi-

fied, and righteousness was imputed to him, because he
believed God. Circumcision was the token of the righteousness which the patriarch received by faith *before* he was
circumcised (vs. 11).

Just as Abraham believed God's word, so must we receive
the righteousness offered us in Christ. Saving faith is reliance upon God's promise of salvation as declared in the
gospel. It implies trust not only in the historic Christ, but
also in the ever living Redeemer. He who is justified believes not only in the death and resurrection of Jesus, but
also in the import of these facts. He believes that Jesus
died because of our own personal transgressions and that
he was raised up for our own personal justification (4:24-
25). In this awareness, faith involves repentance of sin
and results in a change of character and in conduct patterned after the example of Jesus.

The person who is justified by faith is the recipient of
life of a new quality (5:1–8:39). The negative aspect of this
life is freedom from the bondage of sin; the positive aspect
is devotion to the new loyalty which has replaced the old
servitude.

Some persons might conclude erroneously that freedom
from law is freedom from the requirements of its ethical
standards. Paul refutes the idea that abundance of grace
means license to continue in sin (chapter 6). Salvation
by grace does not lead to indifference to the requirements
of holiness. The reception of grace calls for the cessation of
sin. As a result of faith, the old self has been crucified with
Christ (vss. 6-14). Hence the practice of sin is foreign to
the believer, to whom God imparts a new force of action
which enables him to live according to the divine standard
(8:2). Faith in Christ is to be followed by baptism, which

pictures the fact that the believer has died with the Savior and has risen to walk in newness of life (6:3-5).

Paul uses a legal analogy to illustrate the Christian's release from the bond of law: Just as the death of a husband leaves his wife free to marry another man, so the believer is dead to the law through the body of Christ and may be joined to Him who was raised from the dead (7:1-4). This new freedom is liberty of action to live according to the motivation of the Spirit (8:10-14). It is manifested in a triumphant moral life, which is the opposite of the former thralldom (8:4-11).

In Romans 7:14-25, Paul describes the intensity of the struggle with indwelling sin. Certainly he includes himself in this narration which pictures the despair of the human heart. He voices the agony of every man who is in a similar state. But what period of his life is Paul describing? Is the passage an autobiography of Paul the Christian, or is it a reference to his preconversion experience? Scholars are divided on this point. There is no easy solution to the problem, for obstacles are encountered in either view.

Knox thinks Romans 7:14-25 is a description of Paul's inward experience as a Christian. Interpreted thus, Knox would reconcile "the logical incompatibility" of this section with other passages in Paul's letters, in which the Christian life is portrayed in terms of victory over sin, by taking Romans 7:14-25 as an illustration of "a paradoxical character in Paul's thought."[12] Stifler sees the passage as a description of "the state of things prior to the intervention of Christ."[13]

Moffat rearranges the last two verses of Romans 7, in his words, "restoring the second part of verse 25 to what seems

---

[12]Knox and Cragg, *op. cit.*, p. 499.
[13]Stifler, *op. cit.*, p. 133.

its original and logical position before the climax of verse 24."[14] Phillips,[15] Schonfield,[16] and Laubach[17] do likewise.

It must be said that we have no manuscript evidence to support the hypothesis of displacement for Romans 7:25b. Barmby regards the thanksgiving of 7:25a as "a parenthetical expression, anticipating for a moment the purport of ch. viii."[18] Stifler says of Romans 8:1, "The connection by the word 'Therefore' is with the first clause of the preceding verse, and through it with that to which the clause refers."[19]

The idea of servitude in Paul's expression, *having been sold under sin's power* (7:14) is language which reflects the slave market. It is a strong figure in which sin is personified and it apparently depicts the state of an unregenerate person who is bound by fetters which he cannot break. Paul's emphatic phrase, *I myself* in 7:25b, seems to refer to the period in which he lived by his own efforts, i.e. before he met the Savior.

The fact that Paul uses the present tense in Romans 7:14-25 does not necessarily mean that he is describing his condition at the time of writing. The use of the historical present tense to relate graphically a past experience was common among Koinē writers. There are many examples of such a grammatical form in the New Testament. Robertson says, "This vivid idiom is popular in all languages, particularly in the vernacular."[20] Therefore the verbs in Ro-

---

[14]James Moffatt, *The New Testament: A New Translation.*

[15]J. B. Phillips, *Letters to Young Churches,* and *The New Testament in Modern English.*

[16]Hugh J. Schonfield, *The Authentic New Testament.*

[17]Frank C. Laubach, *The Inspired Letters in Clearest English.*

[18]Barmby, *op. cit.,* p. 190.

[19]Stifler, *op. cit.,* p. 135.

[20]A. T. Robertson, *A Grammar of the Greek New Testament in the Light of Historical Research,* p. 866.

mans 7:14-25 may be considered as historical present used
by Paul to describe forcibly his pre-Christian struggle with
indwelling sin.

It is clear that the unregenerate state under the Law is
depicted in Romans 7:3-13. In verse 14, as Paul proceeds
with his narration by changing from the historical tenses to
the present tense, the conjunction *gar, for,* which introduces
the new section, may be interpreted as explanatory and
thus indicates a continuation of the thought of the preceding section. It is also worthy of note that the change of
tense in verse 14 is made while Paul is still speaking of the
Law.

The antithetical statements, "I myself with my better
judgment serve the law of God, but with the old nature
the principle of sin" (7:25b) seem to be a summarization
of the conflict discussed in verses 14-24. R. A. Knox renders
7:25b, "If I am left to myself, my conscience is at God's
disposition, but my natural powers are at the disposition of
sin."[21] Hunter says of Romans, "Chapter vii vividly describes the terrible Jekyll-and-Hyde struggle that goes on
in man until he finds salvation in Christ."[22] Filson remarks
of the passage in question:

Such a note of absolute failure contradicts so completely the picture of victory and growth which we find in the adjoining chapters
that it cannot be taken as a description of the Christian life. It must
be a picture, undoubtedly made more explicit in the light of subse-
quent Christian experience, of the moral futility which Paul saw at-
tended his efforts in his pre-Christian days.[23]

In Romans 8 Paul describes the indwelling of the Holy
Spirit in the Christian. The Spirit imparts to the believer

[21]R. A. Knox, *The New Testament of Our Lord and Saviour Jesus Christ:
A New Translation.*
[22]Hunter, *op. cit.,* p. 94.
[23]Floyd V. Filson, *Pioneers of the Primitive Church,* p. 125.

the nature of the sons of God (8:14-16). This means the present realization of a new order of life and the assurance of future glory. Thus we are heirs, in fact coheirs with Christ (vs. 17). Such right of inheritance may involve hardships for Christ's sake, but when Paul speaks of such suffering it is never in a pessimistic mood. As in 5:3-5, so here again, we see a courageous facing of tribulation which eventuates in hope (8:18-27). Paul is optimistic because, even in the midst of difficult circumstances God is working for good in behalf of those who continue loving Him (vs. 28). No one is able to condemn the believer, for God has justified him on the grounds of the death, resurrection, and intercession of Christ (vss. 33-34). Paul closes the chapter with a magnificent hymn of praise for the gracious love which God has manifested in Jesus Christ, and which is the basis of confidence in ultimate victory (vss. 35-39).

But even as Paul rejoiced in the righteousness which faith brings, he wrestled with a difficult historical problem. Why had the Jews not accepted God's salvation? They had been His chosen people for so long. Many privileges were theirs. They had been especially prepared for the coming of the Christ. Why had the mass of them rejected the Savior? The Jewish attitude placed a heavy burden upon Paul's heart. Had God's promises failed? Had God cast away His people?

Paul devotes chapters 9—11 to this problem, and in each of these chapters one aspect of his threefold answer is set forth:

1. God's word is always effective in the sphere to which it applies. The Apostle argues that God's promises have not failed even though the Jews in general have not received the salvation provided in Christ. He shows that the

saving promise was not made indiscriminately to all the natural progeny of Abraham, but to those who, on the basis of faith, are the true descendants (9:6-8). God's blessing stems from his gracious call,[24] and not because of human works (vss. 9-13). Paul discerns a purpose expressive through history, a purpose working by means of divine selection. To illustrate this point, Paul turns to Jewish history and reviews God's providential dealings with the forefathers. The covenant made with Abraham and Isaac was reconfirmed and continued through the line of Jacob rather than through that of Esau (vss. 9-13).

If it be asked whether such selection is partial, Paul answers that God is absolute sovereign; hence it is His prerogative to do as he wishes with his creations (vss. 14-21). Therefore God has the right to include Gentiles as well as Jews (vss. 22-24), and the prophets Hosea and Isaiah announced the exercise of this right (vss. 25-29). There is no fatalistic predestination in Paul's view, for he concludes that the Gentiles obtained the righteousness conditioned on faith, but that the Jews, following the method of law, fell short (vss. 30-33).

2. The failure lies in the realm of human responsibility. God has not arbitrarily cast away the Jews. God's covenant is presented as a free promise on His part, but its fulfillment hinges upon man's response. There must be a willingness to receive what God offers. Human choice is involved in the final outcome. Israel refused the way of salvation taught by their own Scriptures (10:1-21). Thus Israel's rejection was the result of their own unbelief. There was no lack of opportunity, for the message about faith was announced

---

[24] In Pauline theology, being called of God denotes both the divine invitation and the human acceptance.

everywhere among the Jews. God stretched forth his hand to save them, but they refused his offer (vs. 21).

3. The existence of a remnant proves the integrity of God's promise. The picture is not completely dark, for not all the Jews have refused to believe. At least a remnant, "the election,"[25] i.e. those selected on the basis of faith, has embraced the gospel (11:1-7). Paul, as a believer, was one of the remnant (vs. 1).

The strategy of a remnant was a familiar one in the history of God's people (vss. 2-6). As from time to time a portion of the faithful had survived God's judgments and carried on his work, so now those who are God's people by faith in Christ constitute the nucleus of the new Israel which is spiritual in character (vss. 6-32).

What is Paul saying in Romans 11:26? Does his statement, "And so all Israel shall be saved," predict the final restitution of the Jews as a nation? In Romans Paul refers to Israel in a dual sense. In one instance the word denotes natural Israel, and in another instance it denotes spiritual Israel (9:6). In 11:5-7 Paul makes a distinction between "the election" and "Israel," i.e. between those who by faith have obtained righteousness, and "the rest," i.e. those who, as a result of unbelief, were blinded. Therefore when Paul speaks of the salvation of "all Israel" in the context of 11:26, he means spiritual Israel.[26] This is the only pos-

---

[25]As used by Paul, the Greek terms commonly rendered "predestinate" and "elect" indicate God's plan for mankind; but the divine purpose can be rejected by human unbelief or apostasy. Although we cannot solve the antithesis of divine sovereignty and human freedom, Sanday and Headlam suggest that an answer may be found "in the full acceptance and realization of what is implied by the infinity and the omniscience of God." Cf. *op. cit.*, pp. 347-350.

[26]For a statement of opinions of scholars on this point, see Henry Alford, *The New Testament for English Readers*, pp. 945-946.

sible interpretation in the light of the fact that part of literal Israel experiences hardness (vs. 25).

The Greek word commonly rendered "so" in Romans 11:26 is *houtōs,* an adverb of manner. By his use of it Paul draws an inference from his preceding statement and indicates in what way the action to follow takes place. Thus he describes the manner in which all [spiritual] Israel will be saved: with hardening coming upon and remaining[27] with part of [literal] Israel until the fulfillment of the Gentiles takes place (vs. 25).[28]

The idea of spiritual Israel is in harmony with Paul's overall view that standing with God is a matter of faith. Earlier in the Epistle he has shown that the true children of Abraham are not his physical descendants, but are all who, after Abraham's example, place trust in God's saving promise (4:1-25). It is expressly declared that a person is not a Jew in God's sight unless he has the inward character of a believer (2:28-29). Within this spiritual framework Paul treats the Jewish problem. In Galatians 3:29 he makes the summary statement that the seed of Abraham are all those persons, whether Jews or Gentiles, who have received salvation by faith in Christ. In Paul's thought God's Israel now is composed of spiritual Jews. In Galatians 6:15-16 the Apostle uses the expression, "the Israel of God," to denote the persons who are a new creation in Jesus Christ. Williams renders this passage, "For neither circumcision nor the lack of it has any value, but only a new creation. Now peace and mercy be on all who walk by this rule; that

---

[27]Indicated by Greek perfect tense.

[28]Lenski holds that a national restoration of the Jews is excluded by both the Old and the New Testament. For his discussion see *op. cit.,* pp. 713-734.

is, on the true Israel of God."[29] Laubach also brings out the Apostle's emphasis: "Being circumcised means nothing and not being circumcised means nothing. It is the new birth that means everything. Peace and mercy be upon you who are guided by this higher law. You are the true children of Abraham, the true Israel of God."[30] See also the renderings of Moffatt, the Revised Standard Version, J. B. Phillips, and the Amplified New Testament.

The Apostle concludes his theodicy with a hymn of praise to the riches of God's inscrutable wisdom and knowledge (Rom. 11:33-36).

Paul usually ends his letters on a practical note, and he does so with Romans. After discussing the nature of the righteousness which is appropriated by faith, he shows how it should be demonstrated in Christian behavior.

The first section of ethical emphases (12:1—13:14) is a group of counsels regarding the Christian's relation to God, to other believers, to enemies, and to the civil authority. There is stress upon the supremacy of love in all human relationships, and upon the importance of readiness in view of the proximity of final salvation.

Next Paul gives advice about matters of conscience (14:1—15:13). He is aware of the potential danger which is inherent in a situation where there are scruples based upon an inadequate view of the Christian faith. Persons of stronger or more enlightened conscience might become impatient, treat with contempt their weaker brethren, and entice them to act against their own judgment. Persons of weaker or less enlightened conscience might try to bind their scruples upon the stronger brethren, thus destroying

---

[29]Charles B. Williams, *The New Testament: A Translation in the Language of the People*.
[30]Laubach, *op. cit.*, p. 104.

the latter's liberty. Paul shows that it is wrong for either group to treat the other coercively or critically. He urges all believers to abstain from censure of one another and to leave all judgment to God. He counsels the "weak" not to bind their conscience upon the "strong." He urges the "strong" to bear with the "weak," and not to do anything which might cause a brother to stumble.

Paul's treatment of conscience questions is an example for all time of the application of Christian ethics to congregational life. It is noteworthy that he does not make the weakness of the overscrupulous the criterion of conduct for the church. In the words of Lenski, "Paul refuses to reduce the strong to the level of the weak. The weak ought to grow strong."[31] Scott[32] thinks Paul's greater sympathies were with the strong, and that most of the Apostle's readers were in this category.

In the final section (15:14—16:27) Paul reviews his ministry and announces his plans for the future. In the last chapter is the commendation of Phoebe, salutations, a warning concerning false teachers, and the doxology.

The doxology epitomizes the message of Romans. After introducing his thesis in 1:17 and expounding it in the body of the letter Paul, once more as he terminates the Epistle, reiterates the central truth that righteousness is the result of obedience based on faith. The Apostle is thrilled by the fact that the mystery of salvation, kept silent in the counsel of the omniscient God during long ages, is now made known for the enlightenment and redemption of all peoples. In this grand doxology, to use the words of Hort,

---

[31]Lenski, *op. cit.*, p. 813.
[32]Ernest Findlay Scott, *The Literature of the New Testament*, p. 163.

"the eternal operation of Him 'from Whom, through Whom, and unto Whom are all things,' is translated into the language of history."[33]

OUTLINE

Introduction, 1:1-17.

    1. Apostolic salutation, 1:1-7.

    2. Thanksgiving and statement of purpose, 1:8-15.

    3. Thesis: God's kind of righteousness, 1:16-17.

I. THE UNIVERSAL NEED FOR RIGHTEOUSNESS, 1:18—3:20.

    1. Apart from the Law, the Gentiles are condemned, 1:18-32.

        a. They ignored the revelation given in nature, 1:-18-22.

        b. They became idolatrous, 1:23-25.

        c. They engaged in vile conduct, 1:26-32.

    2. In the sphere of the Law, the Jews are equally guilty, 2:1—3:20.

        a. There is no partiality with God, 2:1-16.

        b. Spiritual experience, not lineage, makes a person a genuine Jew, 2:17-29.

        c. The Law brings awareness of sin, but it has no saving power, 3:1-20.

II. THE CHARACTER OF GOD'S KIND OF RIGHTEOUS-NESS, 3:21—4:25.

    1. It is conditioned on faith, apart from any works of law, 3:21-31.

    2. It is in accord with the Old Testament, 4:1-24.

        a. Illustrated in Abraham and extolled by David, 4:1-8.

        b. Abraham was declared righteous before he was circumcised, 4:9-12.

---

[33]Lightfoot, *op. cit.,* p. 326.

c. The promise made to Abraham's heirs is appropriated by the faith-kind of righteousness, 4:-13-16.

d. The faith required by the gospel is the same in essence as that of Abraham, 4:17-24.

3. It is realized by a sense of personal trust in the merits of Jesus' death and resurrection, 4:25.

III. RESULTS OF GOD'S KIND OF RIGHTEOUSNESS, 5:1—8:39.

1. Justification and peace with God, 5:1-21.

a. On the basis of God's act of love in sending the Holy Spirit and in giving his Son in our behalf, 5:1-11.

b. Through the life-giving obedience of Christ which is in contrast to the death-bringing disobedience of Adam, 5:12-21.

2. Freedom from the dominion of sin, 6:1-23.

a. Baptism pictures the spiritual transformation, 6:1-10.

b. Cessation of the old servitude, 6:11-23.

3. A new relation to law, 7:1-25.

a. The limited jurisdiction of law, 7:1-6.

b. The function of the Law, 7:7-13.

c. The struggle with indwelling sin, 7:14-23.

d. Release from inner conflict, 7:24-25.

4. Participation in the life of the Spirit, 8:1-39.

a. A new force of action, 8:1-11.

b. The blessings of sonship, 8:12-17.

c. Assurance of ultimate glory, 8:18-25.

d. Divine intercession and providence, 8:26-30.

e. The power of Christ's love, 8:31-39.

IV. THE PROBLEM OF JEWISH UNBELIEF, 9:1—11:36.

1. Paul's sorrow for his kinsmen, 9:1-5.

2. Israel's rejection is not inconsistent with God's word, 9:6a-13.

a. The true Israel is determined by faith, 9:6b-9.

b. God works according to his sovereign purpose, 9:10-13.

3. Israel's rejection is not inconsistent with God's justice, 9:14-29.
4. The failure of the Jews is their own fault, 9:30—10:18.
   a. They sought their own righteousness instead of the righteousness of faith, 9:30-33.
   b. Their zeal lacked sufficient knowledge, 10:1-4.
   c. They had many opportunities, but neglected them, 10:5-18.
5. Jewish unbelief was predicted by their own scriptures, 10:19-21.
6. Israel's apostasy is not total, 11:1-36.
   a. A remnant is saved, 11:1-10.
   b. The salvation of Gentiles should challenge Jews to believe, 11:11-17.
   c. Gentiles are not to boast, 11:18-25a.
   d. The manner of Israel's salvation, 11:25b-32.
   e. A hymn of praise to God, 11:33-36.

V. THE PRACTICAL APPLICATION OF RIGHTEOUS-NESS, 12:1—15:13.
   1. The reasonableness of consecration, 12:1-2.
   2. The proper exercise of spiritual gifts, 12:3-13.
   3. The general conduct of a Christian, 12:14-21.
   4. Responsibilities as citizens, 13:1-7.
      a. Government is for human good and has divine sanction, 13:1-5.
      b. Civil structure is to be supported by taxation, 13:6-7.
   5. Love is the supreme principle of behavior, 13:8-10.
   6. The nearness of the final day is a motive for readiness, 13:11-14.
   7. Advice regarding matters of conscience, 14:1—15:13.
      a. Christians should not criticize each other, for the Lord is the judge, 14:1-13.
      b. Christian liberty should be used properly, 14:14-16.
      c. Emphasis should be upon major principles, 14:17-21.
      d. Right action is based on confidence, 14:22-23.
      e. Christ is our example, 15:1-13.

VI. RÉSUMÉ OF PAUL'S PREVIOUS MINISTRY AND FUTURE INTENTIONS, 15:14-33.
1. His principle in choosing fields of labor, 15:14-21.
2. Delays in visiting Rome, 15:22-23.
3. The collection for Jerusalem, and plans regarding Spain, 15:24-33.

VII. CONCLUSION, 16:1-27.
1. Commendation of Phoebe, 16:1-2.
2. Personal salutations, 16:3-16.
3. Caution about false teachers, 16:17-20.
4. Greetings from Paul's co-workers, 16:21-24.
5. The doxology, 16:25-27.

PAUL'S EPISTLE TO THE ROMANS

PART II

AN EXEGETICAL TRANSLATION

TO THE ROMANS

Chapter 1

Paul, a slave of Christ Jesus, a called apostle, in the state of having been set apart for the purpose of [proclaiming] the good news of God, 2which he previously promised through his prophets in writings which by their character are sacred, 3concerning his Son who in relation to humanity became a descendant of David, 4but in relation to deity was declared the Son of God with mighty power by the resurrection from the dead—Jesus Christ our Lord; 5through whom we received divine favor and apostleship to urge among all nations the obedience which faith produces,*a* in behalf of his name, 6among whom you also are called ones of Jesus Christ. 7To all the beloved of God in Rome, constituted saints in response to [God's] call: May divine favor be yours, and peace, from God our Father and [from] the Lord Jesus Christ.

8In the first place, I am giving thanks to my God through Jesus Christ concerning all of you, because [the way in which you are demonstrating] your faith is being broadcast up and down the whole world. 9For God is my witness, to whom I am rendering spiritual service in [devotion to] the gospel of his Son, how unceasingly I make mention of you, 10always in my prayers beseeching that somehow now at last I may be permitted by the will of God to come to you. 11For I wish very much to see you, in order that I may impart to you some spiritual benefit, that you may be firmly established. 12That is to say, that while I am among you, we may be mutually encouraged by each other's faith, yours being a blessing to me and mine to you.

13I want you to know too, [my] brothers, that many times I planned to come to you (but responsibilities elsewhere*b* prevented me), in order that I might gather some fruit among you as well as among other Gentiles.*c* 14Both to Greeks and to barbarians, both to the educated and to the uneducated, I am held by an obligation. 15So, as far as my own willingness is concerned,*d* I am eager to preach the gospel to you in Rome also. 16For I am not ashamed of the gospel: indeed, by its very nature*e* it is God's own power by which he saves every person who is trusting [in the message], both Jew and Greek alike.*f* 17For in it is revealed God's kind*e* of righteousness—[the righteousness] which is entirely by faith,*g* just as it stands written,

---

*a*Rendering *pisteōs, faith,* as subjective genitive.
*b*Cf. 15:20-22.
*c*Or, among the rest of the nations.
*d*Literally, as the [situation] according to me [is].
*e*Implied by anarthrous construction.
*f*Or, the Jew first, but also the Greek.
*g*Greek, "out of faith into faith." Paul emphasizes the fact that righteousness begins and continues in faith.

Now the man who is righteous on the basis of faith shall live.[h]

[18]Certainly the holy wrath of God is constantly being revealed from heaven against all the impiety and unrighteousness of men who in wickedness are suppressing the truth, [19]because that which is known about God is manifest within them: indeed God made it evident to them. [20]For the invisible things of him—both his eternal power and divine nature—ever since the creation of the world have been clearly discernible by means of the things [he] made, so that they are utterly without excuse. [21]Although having been acquainted with God, they did not glorify him as God, nor did they show gratitude, but they became futile in their reasonings and their senseless heart was darkened. [22]Pretending to be wise, they became stupid, [23]and they exchanged the glory of the incorruptible God for a likeness of an image of perishable man, and of w i n g e d creatures, four-footed beasts, and reptiles. [24]So then, because of the sinful cravings of their hearts, God gave them over to uncleanness which resulted in the degrading of their bodies among themselves. [25]They exchanged the truth of God for falsehood, and worshiped and served the creature rather than the Creator who is blessed forever, Amen.

[26]For this reason God abandoned them to passions of dishonor. Actually even their women[i] changed the natural function of sex into that which is contrary to nature. [27]Indeed in like manner also the males, having disregarded the natural function of the females, were inflamed with lust for each other; males engaging in shameful practices with males, and duly receiving in their own persons the retribution which was the inescapable penalty of such error. [28]And inasmuch as they decided not to give proper acknowledgment to God, he gave them over to a mind insensible to reproof, to detestable practices. [29]They reached a state in which they were filled with all unrighteousness, wickedness, covetousness, degeneracy; full of envy, murder, strife, deceit, evil disposition. [30]They were secret slanderers, evil speakers, hateful to God.[j] They delighted in hurting others. They were haughty, boastful, inventors of evil devices, disobedient to parents, [31] void of [spiritual and moral] discernment, untrustworthy, without affection for those who should have been dear to them because of the ties of kinship, having no pity. [32]Although having known well the inexorable mandate of God, that those who engage in such things deserve death, they not only do them, but heartily approve others[k] who practice them.

---

[h]Habakkuk 2:4.

[i]Greek, *thēleiai*, "females." Paul's use of the terms "females" and "males," instead of "women" and "men" in his reference to homosexual vices in verses 26-27, denotes the low level of the immoral practices which he condemns.

[j]Or, haters of God.

[k]Greek, "the ones."

Chapter 2

Therefore you are without excuse, O man, whoever you are, who assumes the role of a critic; for the very fact that you are judging the other person brings condemnation upon yourself because you, the critic, are practicing the things you condemn.*a* 2Now we know that God's verdict is in accordance with truth against those who practice such things. 3And you, O man, who criticizes those who are committing such things, yet all the while doing them [yourself], do you suppose that you*b* will escape the condemnation of God? 4Or do you spurn the wealth of his kindness and toleration and longsuffering, unaware of the fact that such gracious treatment is God's effort*c* to lead you to a change of mind?*d* 5But according to your obstinacy and impenitent heart, you are heaping up retribution against yourself for the day of the wrath and the revelation of the righteous judgment of God, 6who will give every man what is due him according to his deeds: 7eternal life to those who with endurance in good work are seeking glory and honor and immortality; 8but wrath and indignation to those who out of self-interest employ subtle schemes of evasion, and do not obey the truth but are obedient to unrighteousness. 9Extreme distress and inescapable calamity [will come] upon every human soul who persists in practicing evil, upon both Jew and Greek alike;*e* 10but [there will be] glory and honor and peace for every person who is performing the good, for Jew and Greek alike.*f* 11Certainly there is no partiality with God!

12Now as many as sinned without law will also perish without law; and as many as sinned in the sphere of law will be judged by law. 13For it is not the hearers of law who are righteous before God, but the doers of law will be declared righteous. 14Actually, when the Gentiles, who have no law, intuitively do the things required by the law, they, having no law, are a law to themselves. 15They demonstrate the effect of the law written in their hearts, their conscience bearing witness with them, and their moral reflections accusing or else defending them, 16in the day when, according to my gospel, God through Christ Jesus exercises judgment upon the secret things of men.

17Now you who take*g* the name of Jew for yourself,*h* and rely upon law, and boast of God's favor, 18and know his will, and are able to discriminate between moral values,*i* being habitually instructed out of the Law; 19having convinced yourself that you are indeed a guide to the blind, a light

---

*a*Greek, "the same things."
*b*Su, emphatic personal pronoun.
*c*Indicated by conative present tense of verb.
*d*Or, to repentance.
*e*Or, upon the Jew first, but also upon the Greek.
*f*Or, for the Jew first, but also for the Greek.
*g*A condition of reality.
*h*Emphatic *su*.
*i*Or, between things that differ.

to the ones in darkness, 20a corrector of the stupid, a teacher of infants, because you have in the Law the representation of knowledge and of the truth—21you, therefore, who are teaching others, you teach yourself, do you not? You who declare that one should not steal, do you steal? 22You who prohibit adultery, do you commit adultery? You who voice such horror about contamination with idols, do you deal in idolatrous objects for gain?*j* 23You who are making a boast regarding law, do you by transgression of the Law dishonor God? 24Indeed, just as it stands written,

> The name of God is blasphemed among the Gentiles because of you.*k*

25Now anything of the character*l* of circumcision indeed is profitable if you practice the Law; but if you are a transgressor of the Law, your circumcision has reached a state*m* in which it is the equivalent of uncircumcision. 26If, on the other hand, the uncircumcised man keeps the moral requirements of the Law, his uncircumcision will be accounted as the equivalent of circumcision, will it not? 27The man who is physically uncircumcised and yet fulfills the Law will condemn you who have the letter [of the Law] and are physically circumcised, and yet transgress the Law. 28In fact, he is not a Jew who has the outward marks; neither is true circumcision a physical thing; 29but the real Jew is one inwardly, and real circumcision is of the heart, in the spirit, not in the letter. The praise of such an individual comes not from men but from God.

Chapter 3

Then what advantage does the Jew have? Or of what benefit is circumcision? 2Much in every way. First, because the Jews were entrusted with the utterances of God. 3What if some of them did prove unfaithful? Their unfaithfulness does not nullify God's faithfulness, does it? 4By no means! But even if every man is a liar, let God always be true, as it stands written,

> That thou mayest be vindicated
> in thy words, and win the verdict
> any time*a* thou art judged.*b*

5But if our unrighteousness exhibits the righteousness of God, what shall we say? God is not unjust when he inflicts retribution, is he? (I speak according to a human way of thinking.*c*) 6Not at all! If that were true, how could God judge the world? 7Furthermore, if the truth of God abounded to his glory because of my falsehood, why am I still being judged as a sinner? 8And why not say (as we are reproachfully charged, and as some allege that we assert), Let us do evil that good may come? The condemnation of those [who make such an allegation] is just. 9What then? Have we advantage for ourselves? Not in all re-

---

*j*Literally, do you plunder shrines?
*k*Isaiah 52:5, adaptation from the Septuagint.
*l*Qualitative force of anarthrous *peritomē*.
*m*Denoted by perfect tense of verb.
*a*Implied by present infinitive in temporal clause.
*b*Psalm 51:4.
*c*Or, I use an argument such as men would employ.

spects; for we have already brought charge against both Jews and Greeks, that they are all under sin. ¹⁰Thus it stands written:

There is not a righteous person, not even one!

11 No one understands, no one is seeking after God.

12 All have deviated from the right way,

All to a man have become corrupt;

No one habitually does good, not so much as one!

13 Their throat is a grave standing open;

With their tongues they have talked deceitfully;

The poison of deadly serpents is under their lips.

14 Their mouth is full of cursing and bitterness.

15 Their feet are swift to shed blood.

16 Devastation and misery are in their wake,

17 And the way of peace they have not known.

18 There is no reverence of God before their eyes.ᵈ

¹⁹Now we know that whatever the 'Law says, it speaks to those who are within the jurisdiction of the Law, in order that every mouth may be silenced and all the world become liable to God's judgment; ²⁰because no individual will be pronounced righteous before him on the ground of obedience to law. Actually, all law can do is bring a full awareness of sin.

²¹But now God's kind of righteousness stands manifested apart from law [of any kindᵉ], although it is attested by the Law and the Prophets. ²²Indeed God's kind of righteousness is through faith in Jesus Christ. It is effective for all who are trusting [in him]. ²³There is no distinction, for the whole race has sinnedᶠ, and [man] continues to fall shortᵍ of God's standard. ²⁴The permanentʰ principle of justification operates freely by the gift of his grace through the redemption which is in Christ Jesus, ²⁵whom God openly set forth as the means of expiation by his blood, to be appropriated through faith. This was to demonstrate God's righteousness, inasmuch as in his forbearance he had tolerated the previously committed sins. ²⁶He did so, looking forward to the display of his righteousness in the present time, that he might be righteous himself even while declaring righteous the person who places trust in Jesus.ⁱ

²⁷Then what becomes of human boasting? It is shut out completely! On what sort of principle? On that of works? No, but on the principle of faith. ²⁸For we conclude that a man is declared righteous by faith, apart from any works of law. ²⁹Or [is God] the God of the Jews only? [He is the God] of the Gentiles also, is he not? Yes, also of the Gentiles, ³⁰since it is a fact that there is but one God. He will declare righteous the circumcision on the basis of faith, and the uncircumcision by means of faith. ³¹Does

---

ᵈCompounded quotation. Cf. Psalms 5:9; 10:7; 14:1-3; 36:1; 140:3; Isaiah 59:7-8.

ᵉDenoted by anarthrous *nomos*.

ᶠConstative aorist.

ᵍPresent indicative.

ʰForce of present participle.

ⁱObjective genitive.

this mean that we nullify law through[j] this faith? Not at all! Instead, we establish law in its proper place.

Chapter 4

What are we to infer about the status[a] of Abraham our natural forefather? [2]Now if Abraham was declared righteous on the basis of works, he has ground for boasting; but not before God. [3]For what does the Scripture say?

> And Abraham believed[b] God, and his faith was counted to him for righteousness.[c]

[4]Now to the individual who works, the pay is not considered as a favor but as an obligation. [5]But the person who does not rely upon work, but is depending upon him who declares righteous the ungodly, that person's faith is counted for righteousness. [6]Even so, David declares the spiritual well-being of the man to whom God counts righteousness apart from works:

> 7 Supremely happy are they whose lawless acts have been forgiven, whose sins have been covered over!
>
> 8 Supremely happy is the person whose sin the Lord will not at all count against him![d]

[9]Now is this spiritual well-being for the circumcised only, or for the uncircumcised also? We reiterate, Abraham's faith was counted to him for righteousness. [10]Actually in what circumstances was it thus counted? Was it after he was circumcised, or before he was circumcised? It was not after he was circumcised, but before. [11]And he received a sign consisting of circumcision which was a seal to certify the righteousness which was his by faith which he had before he was circumcised, that he might be the father of all who believe, even though they are uncircumcised, that this righteousness might be counted to them; [12]and that he might be the father[e] of those who are not merely circumcised but who also walk in the steps of our father Abraham in the faith which he had prior to circumcision.

[13]For the promise to Abraham or to his posterity that he should be the heir of the world did not come through anything in the category[f] of law, but through the righteousness conditioned on faith. [14]For if those who depend on law be heirs, faith stands emptied of significance and the promise is permanently nullified. [15]Indeed the law continually produces wrath; but where there is no law, neither is there transgression. [16]This is why fulfillment hinges on faith, in order that it might be a matter of unmerited favor, so that the promise might be assured for all the progeny, not only for those [whose background is] of the Law, but also for those who are of the kind of faith exercised

---

[j]Or, by means of.

[a]Force of perfect infinitive of *heuriskō*, "to find."

[b]*Episteuse, he believed,* is placed first in the Greek clause for emphasis.

[c]Genesis 15:6.

[d]Psalm 32:1-2.

[e]Or, circumcision-father.

[f]Force of anarthrous *nomos*.

by Abraham, (who is the father of us all, 17just as it stands written, "I have constituted you the father of many nations,"ᵍ) before him whom he believed, [even before] God who reanimates the dead and who summons nonexistent things as if they already existed. 18In a situation which was hopeless, [Abraham] had hope: he believed that he would become the father of many nations according to the declaration, "Thus shall your descendants be."ʰ 19He never even weakened in faith when he considered the impotent state of his own body—he was about a hundred years old—and Sarah's incapacity for motherhood. 10Indeed, because of the promise of God, he did not waver between certainty and uncertainty, but was empowered by faith. He gave glory [and praise] to God, 21and was fully convinced that what God had promised he was able also to accomplish. 22For this reason [Abraham's faith] was counted to him for righteousness.

23Now it was not because of him only that the statement, "It was counted to him," was written; 24but it was also for our benefit, to whom it is about to be counted, trusting [as we areⁱ] in him who raised from the dead Jesus our Lord, 25who was delivered up because of our misdeeds, and who was raised to life for our justification.

Chapter 5

Therefore having been justified on the basis of faith, let us keep on enjoyingᵃ peace with God through our Lord Jesus Christ, 2by whom also we have obtained the introductionᵇ by faith into this state of divine favor in which we remain standing; and let us continue jubilantᶜ because of our hope of [sharing in] God's glory. 3And not only [do we contemplate future joys], but even in the midst of the [usual] hardships let us go on being jubilant, for we are aware that hardship develops perseverance, 4perseverance [develops] proved character, and proved character [develops] expectation. 5And this expectation never disappoints, because the love of God has been poured forth into and continues inundating our hearts through the Holy Spirit who has been given to us.

6Indeed while we were still weak, Christ at the proper time died in behalf of the ungodly. 7Why, very rarely in behalf of a righteous man will anyone give his life, although in behalf of suchᵈ a good man perhaps someone might even dare to die. 8But God gives proof of his own love for us by the fact that while we were yet sinners, Christ died in our behalf. 9Therefore, since we have now been declared righteous by means of his blood, much more

---

ᵍGenesis 17:5.
ʰGenesis 15:5.
ⁱGreek, "the ones who are trusting."
ᵃRendering *echōmen*, which is present subjunctive.
ᵇOr, access.
ᶜ*Kauchōmetha* is either present indicative or present subjunctive. The latter is hortatory and is in harmony with *echōmen* of verse 1.
ᵈGreek, "the good man."

shall we be saved through him from the wrath [to come]. [10]For if while being enemies we were reconciled to God through the death of his Son, much more, now that we have been reconciled, shall we be saved by his life. [11]And not only so, but we are jubilant continually in God through our Lord Jesus Christ, through whom we have now received this reconciliation.

[12][Look at the situation in this perspective:] Just as through one man sin entered into the world, and through sin came death; even so death passed through to all men, because all men sinned. [13]Certainly sin was in the world prior to the Law, but sin is not charged against a person where there is no law [of any kind]. [14]Nevertheless death reigned from Adam until Moses even over those who did not sin after the likeness of the transgression of Adam,[e] who is a figure of the One who was to come.

[15]But there is a contrast between the misdeed and the gracious gift. For if by the misdeed of that[f] one man the many died, much more did the favor of God and the gift bestowed by grace through the one man, Jesus Christ, abound for the many. [16]Also there is a contrast between the effects of that one man's sin and the effects of the gift. For the sentence occasioned by one man's misdeed was a verdict of condemnation, whereas the gracious gift occasioned by the misdeeds of many results in a verdict of acquittal. [17]For if by the misdeed of the one man death reigned through that one, much more will those who are receiving the abundance of God's[g] favor and his[h] gift of righteousness reign in life through the One, Jesus Christ.

[18]Accordingly then, as through one misdeed condemnation came[i] upon all men, even so through one righteous act there comes[j] to all men life-giving acquittal. [19]For even as by the disobedience of the one man the many were constituted sinners, even so by the obedience of the One the many will be constituted righteous. [20]Law, in addition, came in alongside to accentuate the gravity and enormous scope of the misdeed. But however prevalent and powerful the sum total of sin may be, God's[k] grace has abounded more exceedingly, [21]so that just as sin reigned by death, even so grace might reign by means of righteousness resulting in life eternal through Jesus Christ our Lord.

Chapter 6

What inference then are we to draw? May we remain on in sin in order that God's[a] grace may m u l t i p l y? [2]Away with the

---

[e]Paul seems to mean that they did not violate an explicitly revealed command, as did Adam.

[f]Force of the article.

[g]Greek, "the favor."

[h]Greek, "the gift."

[i]Or, condemnation resulted for all men.

[j]Or, life-giving acquittal resulted for all men.

[k]Implied by the article.

[a]Implied by the article.

thought! How can we, the very persons who[b] died to sin, live in it any longer? [3]Or do you not realize that as many of us as were baptized [as a public declaration of dedication[c]] to Christ Jesus were baptized to picture[d] his death? [4]Therefore we were buried together with him through this baptism which pictures his death, so that just as Christ was raised up from the dead by the glory of the Father, thus we too might demonstrate a new quality of life. [5]For if[e] we have become united with him in the likeness of his death, indeed also we shall be [united with him in the likeness] of his resurrection. [6]This we know, that our former self was crucified with him, in order that the body as the instrument of sin might be rendered inoperative, so that we should no longer go on being slaves of sin. [7]Indeed, the person who has [thus] died stands acquitted of sin. [8]Now in view of the fact that we died with Christ, we believe that we shall also live with him, [9]realizing that Christ, having been raised up from the dead, will never die again; death no longer has any dominion over him. [10]For in his death, he died to sin once [in one consummate, never-to-be-repeated act[f]]; b u t the life he lives, he is living to

God. [11]Thus also you[g] must consider[h] yourselves as dead indeed to sin, but alive to God in Christ Jesus.

[12]Therefore you must not let sin reign in your mortal bodies, causing you to obey their evil desires; [13]neither be presenting your bodily faculties as instruments of unrighteousness in the [service of] sin, but present yourselves now and completely[i] to God as individuals brought from death to life,[j] and [present] your bodily faculties as instruments of righteousness to God. [14]For nothing of the character of sin[k] shall have dominion over you, for you are not under law but under [God's] favor.

[15]In the light of this fact, what is to be our course of action? Shall we commit sin occasionally, because we are not under law but under grace? Certainly not! [16]Do you not realize that to whom you yield yourselves as slaves for obedience, you are slaves of him whom you obey, whether of sin which results in death, or of obedience which results in righteousness? [17]But thanks be to God! Although you were once slaves of sin, you became obedient from your hearts to the standard of doctrine unto which you were delivered, [18]and, having been liberated from sin, you were enslaved to righteous-

---

[b]Rendering *hoitines,* qualitative relative pronoun.

[c]Implied by preposition and context. In the papyri, *eis* was used with *onoma, name,* to denote possession.

[d]Force of *eis,* which in this instance seems to indicate purpose.

[e]A condition of reality.

[f]Denoted by aorist tense and adverb *ephapax,* "only once."

[g]Emphatic *humeis.*

[h]Rendering *logizesthe* as imperative, not indicative.

[i]Force of aorist imperative.

[j]Or, as alive from the dead.

[k]Anarthrous *hamartia.*

ness. 19(I use an analogy from human relations, on account of the weakness of your natural apprehension.) For just as you [previously] surrendered your bodily faculties to the bondage of uncleanness and to more and more lawlessness, so now completely surrender your bodily faculties to the slavery of righteousness for the development*l* of holiness. 20For when you were slaves of sin, righteousness exerted no control over you. 21What was the result of such behavior? Things of which you are now ashamed! For the consummation of those things is death. 22But now, having been set free from sin, and having been enslaved to God, you are bearing the fruit of progress*l* in holiness, and the ultimate destiny is eternal life. 23Mark it well:*m* Sin pays wages in kind, which is death, but the gracious gift of God is life eternal in Christ Jesus our Lord.

Chapter 7
Surely you know, [my] brothers —for I am speaking to persons who understand the nature of law—that the law has jurisdiction over an individual only during the extent of his lifetime! 2For example, a married woman remains bound by law to her husband while he is living; but if her husband dies, she stands completely released from the law regarding the husband. 3Consequently, if she marries another man while her husband is living, she will be desig-

nated an adulteress; but if her husband dies, she is free from his legal claim, so that she is not an adulteress if she marries another man. 4Just so, my brothers, you*a* also were rendered dead to the Law through the body of Christ, so that you might belong to another—to him who was raised up from the dead—in order that we might bring forth fruit for God. 5For when we were motivated by natural impulses, sin's inclinations, irritated by legal restraint, were operative in our bodily faculties, producing a harvest for death. 6But now we have been completely released from the Law, having died [to that] in which we were being held fast, so that we are rendering service in newness of spirit*b* and not in oldness of letter.*c*

7What is the implication of this? Is the Law [itself] bad? Certainly not! However I would not have realized what sin meant had it not been for law. For instance, I would not have been aware of evil desire if the Law had not said, "You must not have evil desire."*d* 8Indeed sin, having obtained a base operation by means of the commandment, aroused in me every kind of illicit desire; for apart from law, sin lay dormant. 9Actually at one time I was alive apart from law; but when the commandment came, sin was stirred into activity and I died. 10And so for me, this very commandment which was intended for

*l*Denoted by noun suffix.
*m*Rendering explicative *gar*.
*a*Emphatic *humeis*.
*b*Or, newness of the Spirit.
*c*Or, oldness of legal code.
*d*Exodus 20:17; Deuteronomy 5:21.

life resulted in death. ¹¹For sin, having received a base of operation by means of the commandment, completely beguiled me and used it to slay me. ¹²So the Law [itself is] holy, and the commandment [is] holy and just and good.

¹³Does this mean that something which is good became death for me? Not at all! But sin, that it might be exposed as sin, worked out death to me through that which is good. Thus, by means of the commandment, the utterly horrible nature of sin becomes evident. ¹⁴For we know that the Law is spiritual, but I am*e* constituted of weak human nature, in the state of having been sold under sin's power. ¹⁵Actually I am perplexed by my own behavior: for I am not doing what I want to do, but I am practicing what I hate. ¹⁶But if I practice what I do not want to do, I acknowledge that the Law is excellent. ¹⁷In fact, it is not I myself committing such things, but [it is] the indwelling sin within me. ¹⁸For I know that in me, that is in my unregenerate nature, nothing good dwells. The will to do right is constantly with me, but the performance of it is not. ¹⁹Indeed, I am not doing the good that I want to do, but I am practicing the evil that I do not want to do. ²⁰But if I am practicing what I do not want to do, it is really not I myself doing it, but the sin which is dwelling in me. ²¹Accordingly I find this antipathy:*f* although I want to practice the good, the evil is constantly present with me. ²²Certainly in my inmost self I endorse God's Law, ²³but I find another principle of a different kind operating in my bodily faculties, warring against the force of my reason, and bringing me into captivity to the power of the sin which is expressive in my bodily faculties. ²⁴What a miserable man I am! Who will deliver me from this death which enslaves the body?*g* ²⁵Thanks be to God [who gives deliverance] through Jesus Christ our Lord! Accordingly then,*h* I myself with my better judgment serve the Law of God, but with the old nature the principle of sin.

Chapter 8

Consequently there is now no condemnation whatsoever for those who are in Christ Jesus. ²For the principle*a* of the Spirit of life in Christ Jesus has liberated you*b* from the principle*a* of sin and death. ³Indeed, what was impossible for the Law—because it continued weak, being limited by human nature which was the medium in which it had to function—[God accomplished], having sent his own Son in the likeness*c* of sinful nature, and concerning sin,

*e*In verses 14-25, Paul uses the present tense, probably for vividness.

*f*Rendering *nomos* in this context of opposing laws, i.e. forces of action.

*g*Literally, from the body of this death.

*h*Verse 25b seems to be a summary statement of the conflict described in the preceding verses.

*a*Or, force of action.

*b*Second person singular. Some manuscripts have *me*.

*c*Paul is saying that Christ came to share our nature, apart from its sinfulness.

overcame[d] sin in human nature, [4]in order that the righteous requirement of the Law might be fully met in us who do not live by the impulses of the old nature, but by [the motivation of] the Spirit. [5]For individuals who are living according to the old nature have sensual inclinations, but those [who are] living according to the Spirit have spiritual inclinations. [6]The attitude prompted by the old nature [means] death, but the attitude prompted by the Spirit [means] life and peace. [7]Now the attitude prompted by the old nature is hostility toward God; for it does not subject itself to the Law of God—indeed it cannot. [8]Hence it is impossible for people who are dominated by the old nature to please God.

[9]But you[e] are not dominated by the old nature but by the Spirit, if it is a fact that the Spirit of God is dwelling in you. And if any person does not have the Spirit of Christ, such a person[f] is not of him. [10]But if Christ is in you, then although death is inevitable for the body[g] because of sin, yet the spirit[h] [is] life because of righteousness. [11]And if the Spirit of him who raised Jesus from the dead is dwelling in you, he who raised Christ Jesus from the dead will also reanimate your mortal bodies through[i] his Spirit who is dwelling in you.

[12]So then, [my] brothers, we are not obligated to the old nature, to live under its control. [13]For if you live under the control of the old nature, you are heading straight for impending doom;[j] but if by the Spirit you keep putting to death the [improper] deeds of the body, you will continue to live. [14]For as many as are being led by the Spirit of God, these are the sons of God. [15]Indeed you did not receive a spirit of bondage, [to place you] again into [an attitude of] dread; but you received the spirit[k] of sonship in which[l] we exclaim, "O God, our Father!" [16]The Spirit Himself gives witness together with the witness of our spirit that we are children of God. [17]And if children, also heirs— God's heirs and Christ's coheirs— if we really share his sufferings, so that we may also share his glory.

[18]Actually I regard the sufferings of this present period unworthy of consideration in view of the glory about to be unveiled with reference[m] to us. [19]Indeed the creation, with head stretched forward in anticipation, is awaiting eagerly the unveiling of the sons of God. [20]For the creation was subjected to frustration, not

[d]Or, condemned.
[e]The pronoun is emphatic.
[f]Greek, "this one."
[g]Literally, the body [is] dead.
[h]Or, Spirit.
[i]Some manuscripts read, "because of his Spirit," etc.
[j]Greek, "you are about to die."
[k]Or, the Spirit.
[l]Or, by whom.
[m]Rendering preposition, *eis*.

by its own choice, but on account of him who subjected [it]. 21[But this was done] in hope, because even the creation itself will be liberated from the bondage of decay [and will be brought] into the glorious freedom of the children of God. 22For we know that the whole creation continues groaning together and sharing birth pangs until now. 23And not only that, but even we ourselves, who have the Spirit[n] as the foretaste[o] [of the future glory], are inwardly groaning while awaiting attentively [the culmination of] sonship, the redemption of our bodies. 24Indeed in this[p] hope we were saved. A hope seen is not hope, for who hopes for what he sees? 25But if we hope for what we do not see, we wait eagerly for it with endurance.

26Likewise also the Spirit gives assistance in our weakness—he takes hold [of our problems] on the other side[q]—for we do not know what we should pray for as we ought, but the Spirit himself intercedes in our behalf in the groanings which are unutterable. 27And the Searcher of hearts knows the intercessory purpose of the Spirit, that according to [the will of] God he pleads in behalf of [his] consecrated ones.[r] 28And

we know that for those who continue loving God, for those who are the called ones[s] according to [his] purpose, he manipulates[t] all things for good. 29Those whom he foreapproved, he also planned in advance to be conformed to the image of his Son, that he might be the Ideal Representative[u] [as the first to rise from the dead] among many brothers. 30And those whom he planned in advance, he also called; and those whom he called, he also declared righteous; and those whom he declared righteous, he also glorified.

31What therefore are we to conclude in view of these things? If God is for us, who [can be] against us? 32Will not he who went as far as not to spare his own Son, but delivered him up in behalf of us all, also with him freely give us all things [in the whole sphere of salvation]?[v] 33Who can bring any charge against God's chosen ones? God is the one who declares righteous! 34Who can condemn [us]? Is it Christ Jesus who died, and beyond that was raised up, who is at the right hand of God, and who is actually interceding in our behalf? 35What can separate us from the love which Christ[w] has

---

[n]Appositional genitive.

[o]Literally, "firstfruits." In the papyri *aparchē* has such meanings as "entrance fee" and "birth certificate."

[p]Implied by article.

[q]Rendering *sunantilambanetai*, present indicative of double compound verb which means "to take hold at the opposite end together with."

[r]Or, saints.

[s]In Pauline theology, the "called" denotes those who have both heard and accepted God's invitation.

[t]Or, he works together.

[u]Literally, the Firstborn.

[v]Greek, "the all things."

[w]Subjective genitive.

for us? Can hardship, or distress, or persecution, or famine, or nakedness, or peril, or sword? 36As it stands written:

For thy sake we are being put to death all day long; we were regarded as sheep doomed to slaughter.*x*

37But in all these things we are winning a decisive victory through him who loved us. 38For I stand fully convinced that neither death, nor life, nor angels, nor rulers, nor things present, nor things to come, nor powers, 39nor any dimension of space,*y* nor anything in all creation will be able to separate us from the love of God which is in Christ Jesus our Lord!

Chapter 9

I am speaking the truth in Christ—I do not falsify, [for] my conscience, with the Holy Spirit's testimony, bears me witness—2that I have great grief and unceasing sorrow in my heart. 3Actually I was on the point of wishing even myself accursed from the Christ in place of*a* my brethren, my natural kinsmen, 4they who are Israelites, to whom belonged the privileges of sonship, and the [Shekinah] glory, and the covenants, and the giving of the Law, and the temple service, and the promises, 5and the patriarchs, and

from whom, from the standpoint of human descent, came the Christ who is over all, God blessed forever. Amen.

6But this is not implying that the word of God has reached a state of ineffectiveness. Indeed, not all those who descended from Israel constitutes [the true] Israel, 7nor are they all Abraham's children [in the sense of heirs] because they descended from him; but [the promise was], "In Isaac shall offspring be named for thee."*b* 8That is to say, those who are natural descendants are not [thereby] the children of God, but those designated children by the promise are considered [Abraham's] offspring. 9For this statement is a promise:*c* "I will intervene, and about this time next year Sarah shall have a son."*d* 10Furthermore, there is also [the incident of] Rebecca who was with child by Isaac our forefather. 11[Although the same man*e* was the father of both children,] before the twin sons*f* were born or had done anything good or bad, in order that God's purpose of choice might remain, 12which depends not on human works but on the One calling, it was said to her, "The greater shall serve the lesser."*g* 13Thus it stands written:

---

*x*Psalm 44:22.

*y*Literally, nor height nor depth.

*a*Or, in behalf of.
*b*Genesis 21:12.
*c*Greek, *epaggelias*, is emphatic by being placed first in the sentence.
*d*Genesis 18:10, 14.
*e*Indicated by *ex henos*, "of one [husband]," vs. 10.
*f*Indicated by masculine plural participles, *gennēthentōn*, "were born," and *praxantōn*, "had done," in light of original account of twins in Genesis 25: 22-24.
*g*Genesis 25:23.

Jacob I loved, but Esau I hated.*h*

14What then are we to infer? There is no injustice with God, is there? Unthinkable! 15Indeed, he says to Moses:

I will have mercy on whomsoever I have mercy,
And I will have compassion on whomsoever I have compassion.*i*

16Accordingly, therefore, mercy is not [a matter] of man's*j* resolve or effort, but of God who extends it. 17For the Scripture says of Pharaoh:

I have raised you up for the express purpose of displaying my power in [connection with] you,
And to proclaim my name in all the earth.*k*

18Thus [God] has mercy on whom he will, and he hardens whom he will.

19Then you will ask me, Why does he still go on blaming [men for their deeds]? Actually who can maintain resistance against his resolve? 20But the question really is, Who are you, a mere man, to engage in controversy with God? The thing formed does not say to the one having formed it, Why did you make me like this, does it? 21Has not the potter authority over the clay to make out of the same mass one vessel for an honorable use and another for a dishonorable use? 22Then what if God, although willing to manifest his wrath and to make known his power, tolerated with much long-suffering the objects of indignation even though they were in a state of readiness for destruction, 23and [did so] in order to make known the riches of his glory upon the objects of mercy, which he previously prepared for glory, 24even us whom he has called, not only from among the Jews but also from among the Gentiles? 25As, in fact, he says in Hosea:

A people which were not mine, I will call my people;
And her who was not beloved, [I will call] beloved.

26 And in the place where it was said to them, "You are not my people,"
There they shall be called sons of the living God.*l*

27Moreover Isaiah exclaims concerning Israel:

Although the number of the sons of Israel be as the sand of the sea, only the remnant will be saved;

28 For completely and speedily will the Lord accomplish his word upon the earth.*m*

29Also as Isaiah previously said:

If the Lord of hosts had not left us survivors, we would have become like Sodom, and would have resembled Gomorrah.*n*

30What conclusion do we reach? That Gentiles, who were not pursuing righteousness, have

---

*h*Malachi 1:2-3. There is no animosity with God. "I hated" is an anthropopathic expression which refers to the result of divine selection. God may be said to "love less" only by comparison in the sense that Esau was not made the third patriarch.

*i*Exodus 33:19.

*j*Or, one's.

*k*Exodus 9:16.

*l*Hosea 1:10; 2:23.

*m*Isaiah 10:22-23; 28:22.

*n*Isaiah 1:9.

grasped it,[o] even the righteousness conditioned on faith; [31]whereas Israel, pursuing a law characterized by righteousness, did not attain to [such] a law. [32]Why? Because [they sought it] by works rather than by faith. They tripped over the stumbling-stone, [33]just as it stands written:

> Behold I place in Zion a stone of stumbling and a mighty Rock of impediment;
> But the one who trusts in Him will not be put to shame.[p]

Chapter 10

Brethren, that which would give my heart the greatest satisfaction, and that for which I pray to God on behalf [of my kinsmen], is [their] salvation. [2]Of course I can testify that they have zeal for God, but it is [zeal] not based upon sufficient knowledge. [3]For, repudiating[a] God's righteousness, and seeking to establish their own, they did not yield themselves to the righteousness of God. [4]Indeed, Christ is the fulfillment [of everything in the whole realm[b]] of law for righteousness to every individual who is trusting [in him].

[5]Moses writes[c] that the man who can perform the righteousness required by law will live by [that righteousness[d]]. [6]But the righteousness which faith produces speaks thus: Do not say in your heart, Who will ascend into heaven? (that is, to bring Christ down) [7]or, Who will descend into the abyss? (that is, to bring Christ up from the dead). [8]But what does it say? The utterance is near you, on your lips, even in your heart[e] (that is, the utterance about faith which we are proclaiming): [9]If you acknowledge with your mouth that Jesus is Lord, and believe in your heart that God raised him from the dead, you will be saved. [10]For with the heart a person exercises faith that brings righteousness, and with the mouth he makes the acknowledgment that brings salvation. [11]For the Scripture says: "No one who trusts in him will be put to shame."[f] [12]Indeed there is no distinction between Jew and Greek, for the same universal Lord is abounding in resources [accessible] to all who call upon him. [13]For absolutely[g] everyone who calls upon the name of the Lord will be saved.[h]

[14]But how can men call upon him in whom they have not believed? And how can they believe in him of whom they have not heard? And how can they hear unless someone preaches? [15]And how can they preach unless they are sent with a commission? As it stands written:

[o]Greek, "righteousness."
[p]Isaiah 8:14; 28:16.
[a]Or, not knowing; here in the sense of disregarding.
[b]Force of anarthrous *nomos*.
[c]Leviticus 18:5.
[d]Indicated by pronoun *autēi*, in agreement with *dikaiosunēn*.
[e]Deuteronomy 30:11-14.
[f]Isaiah 28:16.
[g]Implied by *hos an*, which is emphatic.
[h]Joel 2:32.

How welcome is the coming[i] of those who announce the glad tidings of good things![j] [16]But not all obeyed the glad news. Indeed, Isaiah asks, **Lord, who has believed our message?**[k] [17]So then, faith [comes] from what is heard, and what is heard [comes] through the utterance about Christ. [18]But I ask, It was not that they never heard, was it? Of course they heard!

> Their sound went forth into all the earth,
> And their utterances into the extremities of the habitable world.[l]

[19]Again I ask, Israel did not fail to know, did they? First, Moses says:

> I myself will make you jealous by those who are no nation;
> By a people without understanding, I will anger you.[m]

[20]Moreover, Isaiah is daring enough to say:

> I was found by those not seeking me;
> I became manifest to those not inquiring for me.[n]

[21]But of Israel he says:

> All day long I stretched forth my hands to a disobeying and recalcitrant people.[o]

Chapter 11

I ask, therefore, God did not thrust away from himself his people, did he? Certainly not! Why,

I myself am an Israelite, a descendant of Abraham, of the tribe of Benjamin. [2]God did not thrust away from himself his people whom he foreapproved. Surely you know what the Scripture says in the passage about Elijah, how he pleads with God against Israel:

> [3] Lord, they have killed thy prophets,
> They have dug down thy altars;
> I am the only one left, and they are seeking my life.[a]

[4]But what does the divine response say to him?

> I have left back for myself seven thousand men who have never bowed a knee to Baal.[b]

[5]Likewise, even in the present period there has come to be a remnant, selected on the principle of [God's] gracious favor. [6]But if it is by [his] gracious favor, it is certainly not on the basis of works; otherwise favor loses its character as favor.

[7]Then what are we to infer? Israel has never obtained that which it is still seeking, but the chosen ones have obtained it. [8]The rest have been hardened, just as it stands written:

> God gave them over to an attitude marked by stupor,
> Eyes that cannot see,
> And ears that cannot hear,
> Even to this day.[c]

---

[i]Literally, how beautiful are the feet.
[j]Isaiah 52:7.
[k]Isaiah 53:1.
[l]Psalm 19:4.
[m]Deuteronomy 32:21.
[n]Isaiah 65:1.
[o]Isaiah 65:2.
[a]1 Kings 19:10.
[b]1 Kings 19:18.
[c]Isaiah 29:10; Deuteronomy 29:4.

⁹And David says:

> Let their table become a
> snare and a hunting net,
> Their death-trap trigger and
> their retribution.
> 10 Let their eyes be darkened so
> they cannot see,
> And their back bent down
> continually.ᵈ

¹¹Now what? The only result of their stumbling was not that they fell, was it? Certainly not! On the contrary, their falling aside [was made the occasion of] salvation for the Gentiles, and should incite [the Jews] to seek a similar blessing.ᵉ ¹²Now if their falling aside [contributed to] the enrichment of the world, and their defection [contributed to] the enrichment of the Gentiles, how much more their fulfillment!

¹³Now I say to you who are Gentiles: Inasmuch as I myself am an apostle of the Gentiles, I seek to accomplish the utmost through my ministry, ¹⁴hoping by this means to stir to jealous rivalry my own kinsmen and [thus] to save some of them. ¹⁵For if their rejection [has resulted in] the reconciliation of the world, what would their reception [mean] but life from the dead? ¹⁶If the first portion of dough [of the heave offeringᶠ] is holy, so also is the lump; and if the root is holy, so also are the branches.

¹⁷Now if some of the branches were broken off, and you, being [of the stock of] a wild olive tree, were grafted in among them, and have become a partaker of the rich sap of the [cultivated] olive's root, ¹⁸do not be boasting against the branches. But if you inclined to feel superior, [bear in mind that] you do not support the root, but the root supports you. ¹⁹You will reply, Branches were broken off so that I on my part might be grafted in! ²⁰Not exactly. They were broken off because of unbelief, and [it is only] by faith that you yourself remain standing. Stop being conceited, but maintain an attitude of reverential fear.ᵍ ²¹For if God did not spare the natural branches, he certainly will not spare you. ²²Therefore you should be aware of the kindness and the sternness of God—upon those who have fallen, sternness; but upon you his kindness, if you continue [to trust] in that kindness; otherwise you too will be cut off. ²³And even the others, if they do not remain in their unbelief, will be grafted in; for God is able to graft them in again. ²⁴For if you were cut out from an essentially wild olive tree and, contrary to nature, you were grafted into a cultivated olive tree, how much easier it should be to graft these natural [branches] into their own olive tree!

²⁵To prevent you from too much presumption, [my] brothers, I want you to understand this revealed secret: hardening in the case of many has come upon Israel and it will continueʰ until the fulfillment of the Gentiles takes place; ²⁶and after this

---

ᵈPsalm 69:22-23.

ᵉLiterally, incite them to jealousy, or to envious rivalry.

ᶠCf. Numbers 15:19-21.

ᵍOr, be afraid [of falling away through unbelief].

ʰImplied by gegonen, perfect tense.

manner all Israel[i] will be saved, just as it stands written:

From out of Zion the Deliverer will come,
He will turn ungodliness away from Jacob;
27 And this is my covenant with them,
When I take away their sins.[j]

28From the standpoint of the gospel, [the Jews] are enemies for your sake; but from the standpoint of [God's original] selection, they are beloved on account of their forefathers. 29For God is not subject to regret with regard to his gracious gifts and his call. 30Even as you[k] were once disobedient to God, but now have been shown mercy on the occasion of their disobedience, 31thus they also now have disobeyed on the occasion of the mercy shown you, in order that they too may now be shown mercy. 32For God has shut up together [in one category] all men because of [their] disobedience, so that he might show mercy to them all.

33O the depth of the riches and of the wisdom and of the knowledge of God![l] How unsearchable [are] his decisions, and how inscrutable his ways!

34 For who has ever comprehended the Lord's thoughts? Or who has ever become his counsellor?

35 Or who has ever first given God anything, and thus put God under obligation to pay him back?[m]
36Because all things have their origin in him, and exist through him, and are for him! To him be glory forever! Amen.

Chapter 12

Therefore I exhort you, [my] brothers, by means of the compassions of God, to present completely your entire selves[a] as a living sacrifice, holy and well-pleasing to God, for this is your reasonable service. 2Do not let this age be setting the pattern for your behavior, but continue being transformed by the renewing of your thinking power, so that you keep discerning what is God's will— [what is] good and well-pleasing and complete.

3Through the divine favor having been given to me, I ask every person among you not to overestimate himself [or his abilities[b]], but to cultivate an attitude of discretion in accordance with the measure of faith which God has apportioned to each one. 4For just as we have many organs in one [human] body, and all the organs do not have the same function, 5so we, who are many [believers], are one body in Christ, and we

---

[i]Spiritual Israel. In this Epistle Paul uses Israel in a dual sense, e.g. 2:28-29; 9:6-8.

[j]Isaiah 59:20-21. Paul quotes loosely from the Septuagint. The Hebrew of Isaiah 59:20 brings out clearly the fact that repentance on the part of Israel is a prerequisite to God's forgiveness and blessing. See the rendering of the Hebrew in the Authorized, English Revised, and Revised Standard Versions.

[k]Emphatic *humeis*.

[l]Or, O the depth of the riches, both of the wisdom and of the knowledge of God!

[m]Isaiah 40:13; Job 35:7; 41:11.

[a]Literally, your bodies.

[b]Implied by context.

are individually members of each other. 6Now we have [certain] gifts that differ according to the divine favor which has been granted to us. [Let each recipient render proper service in the field in which he is qualified.] If [one's gift is] prophecy, [let it be exercised] according to the proportion of his faith.c 7If it is service, [let it be exercised] in service. If it is teaching, [let it be exercised] in teaching. 8If it is exhortation, [let it be exercised] in exhortation. The one who shares [material things should do so] with liberality. The one who presides [should do so] with enthusiasm. The one who renders deeds of kindness [should do so] with cheerfulness.

9[There must be absolutely] no hypocrisy with regard to love. Constantly abhor that which is wicked. Always cling to the good. 10Be devoted to one another in brotherly love, [as members of the same family]. Take the lead in giving honor to e a c h other. 11Never let up in zeal. Keep on fire with the Spirit. Be constantly devoted to the service of the Lord, 12rejoicing in hope, patient in hardship, steadfastly continuing in prayer, 13sharing with the saints who are in need, always practicing hospitality.

14Seek the best interests of those who persecute you; strive for their well-being, and do not invoke evil [upon them]. 15Rejoice with persons who rejoice, and weep with persons who weep. 16Cultivate the attitude of mutual understanding for each other. Do not be haughty, but give yourselves to [the needs of] humble people. Do not become self-opinionated. 17Never return evil for evil to anyone. Take careful forethought [about your conduct]; let it be proper in the presence of everyone. 18If possible, as far as the responsibility is yours, be at peace with everybody. 19Do not avenge yourselves, beloved, but leave place for [God's] wrath, for it stands written:

Vengeance belongs to me; I myself will pay [them] back, saith the Lord.d

20So [as opposed to seeking revenge], if your enemy is hungry, give him food; if he is thirsty, give him something to drink. For by such action you may induce him to repent.e 21Do not allow any evil person or thingf to overcome you from time to time, but keep overcoming the evil by means of the good.

Chapter 13

Let every individual be submissive to the ruling [civil] authorities; for there is no authority except by [the sanction of] God, and the existing [authorities] stand established by him. 2Consequently he who sets himself against the authoritiesa has reached a state of

cOr, in agreement with the faith.
dDeuteronomy 32:35.
eAn interpretive rendering from the idea that "coals of fire" (Greek) cause pain and perhaps a change of mind.
fKakou, "evil," here is either masculine or neuter. Its second use in this verse is neuter.

aThe Greek is singular because Paul states a principle.

resistance against God's arrangement; and those who have reached such a state of resistance will receive judgment upon themselves. [3]For rulers [as a class[b]] are not a terror to good conduct but to evil. Now do you wish to have no fear of the authority? Practice doing good, and you will receive commendation from it; [4]for it is God's agent for your good. But if you are an evil doer, [you have reason to] be afraid; for it is not for nothing that he bears the sword. In fact, he is an instrument of divine order to inflict God's wrath upon the one who practices evil. [5]So you must remain in subjection, not only to avoid this wrath, but also for the sake of conscience. [6]This is the reason why you are paying taxes, for public officials are [servants] of God [in] steadily giving their energies to this ministration.[c] [7]Pay them all that which is due to them —taxes to the [collector of] taxes, revenue to the [collector of] revenue, respect to whom respect [is due], honor to whom honor [is due].

[8]Owe no person anything, except the purposive good will [patterned after the example of Christ] which is our perpetual[d] debt to each other. He who continues demonstrating this good will[e] to his fellowmen is in the state of having fully met the requirements of [the entire category[f] of] law. [9]For

[the commandments], You must not commit adultery, You must not kill, You must not steal, You must not have evil desire, and whatever other command of a different kind there may be—all are summed up in this principle: You must love[g] your neighbor as yourself. [10]This purposive good will does not work any harm to its neighbor; therefore it is the fulfillment [of everything in the whole realm[f] of law.

[11]And let us live like this, realizing the significance of the time period, that it is already the hour for you to be aroused from sleep; for now is our [ultimate] salvation nearer than when we first believed. [12]The night has almost ended; the day has drawn near. So let us thoroughly and completely[h] put away from ourselves the deeds of darkness, and let us once and for all[h] put on the full equipment of the light. [13]Let us conduct ourselves honorably, as in the day, not indulging in revellings and drunken sprees, not in illicit sexual intimacies and excesses like people who have lost their sense of shame, [and] not in contention and jealousy. [14]But be clothed with the Lord Jesus Christ, and do not entertain any forethought for [the expression of] any desires of the old nature.

Chapter 14

Now make it a practice to receive to yourselves him whose

---

[b]Denoted by the article.

[c]Literally, to this very thing.

[d]From the present infinitive of *agapaō*. The cognate noun is *agapē*, the sacrificial, redemptive love revealed in Christ.

[e]Present participle.

[f]Implied by anarthrous *nomos*.

[g]Imperative future of *agapaō*.

[h]Force of aorist subjunctive.

faith is weak [due to lack of moral discernment[a]], but not for arguments over opinions. [2]One man has sufficient confidence to eat any kind of food;[b] another, being overscrupulous, eats [only] vegetables. [3]Let the man who eats [any kind of food] stop treating with contempt the man who abstains; and let the one who abstains stop criticizing the one who eats; for God has fully received him.[c] [4]Just who are you[d] to be judging a servant of someone else? To his own lord he stands or falls; but he will be made to stand, for the Lord is able to make him stand.

[5]One person considers a [certain] day more important than another day; someone else considers every day alike. Let each individual be fully assured in his own mind. [6]He who esteems the day esteems it to the Lord. He who eats [any kind of food] does so to the Lord, for he gives thanks to God. And he who abstains does so to the Lord, and he gives thanks to God. [7]Indeed, no one of us lives to himself, and no one dies to himself. [8]If we live, we live to the Lord; and if we die, we die to the Lord. So whether we live or whether we die, we belong to the Lord. [9]This is why Christ died and came to life, that he might become Lord of both the dead and the living. [10]Why, then, do you[e]

[the scrupulous person[f]] go on criticizing your brother? Or also why do you[e] [the unscrupulous person[f]] continue treating your brother with contempt? Actually we must all appear before the judgment seat of God. [11]For it stands written:

As surely as I live, declares the Lord, before me every knee shall bend,
And every tongue shall make full acknowledgment to God.[g]

[12]This means that each one of us will have to answer for himself to God.

[13]Therefore let us cease the habit of passing judgment on one another. Instead, make it your permanent determination[h] not to be setting up anything of the character of a stumbling block or a snare for your brother. [14]I know and stand persuaded in the Lord Jesus that nothing is unclean in itself; it is unclean only to the individual who regards it as unclean. [15]If because of food your brother is grieved, you are no longer acting according to [the norm of] purposive good will.[i] Stop destroying, by means of your food, that person in whose behalf Christ died! [16]You[j] have the [supreme] good; let it not be blasphemed. [17]Indeed the kingdom of God is not [a matter of] eating and drinking, but [it is] righteous-

[a]Implied by context.
[b]Greek, "all things."
[c]Or, received him [unto Himself].
[d]Emphatic by personal pronoun and position in sentence.
[e]Emphatic by personal pronoun and prolepsis.
[f]Indicated by verse 3.
[g]Isaiah 45:23.
[h]Greek, "judge once for all" (aorist imperative).
[i]*Agapē*.
[j]Plural, which seems to denote the whole church.

ness and peace and joy in the Holy Spirit. 18Certainly whoever in this serves the Christ is well pleasing to God and is of tested worth before men.

19Accordingly, therefore, we are pursuing[k] the things of peace and the things that promote mutual upbuilding. 20Stop tearing down[l] God's work for the sake of food! All things [in the classification of food] are indeed [ceremonially] clean; but [anything] is bad for the man who is a stumbling block by what he eats. 21The expedient course is not to eat [the] flesh [of a sacrificial animal], nor to drink wine, nor [to do] anything by which your brother stumbles. 22The confidence which you[m] have with reference to yourself,[n] be having [it] in the sight of God. Truly happy is the man who does not condemn himself in what he tests and approves. 23But the man who hesitates in uncertainty stands condemned if he eats, because [his action] is not based on confidence, and any [action] not based on confidence is sin.

Chapter 15

Now we who are strong [in matters of conscience] ought[a] to bear with the weaknesses of those who are not strong, and not to go on pleasing ourselves. 2Let each one of us try to please his neighbor with regard to the good, with a view to [his] spiritual advancement. 3Most certainly the Christ did not please himself, but as it stands written [of him]:

The reproaches of those who reproach Thee have fallen upon me.[b]

4All the things previously written were recorded for our instruction, in order that through the perseverance and through the encouragement which the Scriptures give[c] we might maintain our hope. 5Now may God, who is the source of this perseverance and of this encouragement, grant you constant unanimity of thought in accordance with [the standard revealed in] Christ Jesus, 6so that with oneness of purpose in one voice you may continue glorifying the God and Father of our Lord Jesus Christ.

7Therefore have the habit of receiving each other to yourselves, even as also the Christ has received us[d] to himself for the glory of God. 8What I mean is that Christ stands constituted a minister to circumcised people,[e] in vindication of God's truthfulness,

[k]Some manuscripts have present subjunctive, Let us pursue.
[l]The imperative is singular, indicating that a particular group is addressed.
[m]Emphatic by pronoun and prolepsis.
[n]Or, to your rule [of behavior].
[a]*Opheilomen, we are under obligation,* is placed first in the sentence for emphasis.
[b]Psalm 69:9.
[c]Or, in order that through the perseverance which the Scriptures [induce in us] through the counsel which they [enjoin upon us] we might continue to have hope.
[d]Some manuscripts read *humas,* "you."
[e]Or, a minister of circumcision.

that he might confirm the promises [given to] the fathers,*f* [9]and that the Gentiles might glorify God on account of his mercy, just as it stands written:

> Therefore I will fully confess Thee among the Gentiles;
> And to the accompaniment of a stringed instrument I will sing praises to Thy name.*g*

[10]And again it declares:

> Rejoice, O Gentiles, with his people!*h*

[11]And again:

> Praise the Lord, all the Gentiles;
> Yea, let all peoples extol him!*i*

[12]And furthermore Isaiah declares:

> The Scion of Jesse will come,
> Even he who rises up to rule the Gentiles;
> On him the Gentiles will place their hope.*j*

[13]Now may God, who is the source of this hope, fill you with all joy and peace as you go on exercising faith, so that you may be overflowing with this hope by the power of the Holy Spirit.

[14]I myself am fully confident regarding you, my brothers, that you yourselves are full of goodness, [that you are] in the state of having been filled with all [essential] knowledge, competent even to admonish one another. [15]But, just as an additional reminder to you, I have written rather boldly on some points*k* because of the gracious favor God

has bestowed upon me [16]in appointing me a public servant of Christ Jesus to the Gentiles. [Thus I am] engaged in the sacred service of the gospel of God, in order to bring about the presentation of the Gentiles as an acceptable offering —[an offering] in the state of having been sanctified by the Holy Spirit.

[17]Therefore I have [basis for] glorying in Christ Jesus concerning the things relating to [the service of] God. [18]I will not presume to mention anything except that which Christ has accomplished through me for the purpose of bringing the Gentiles*l* to obedience. [19][He wrought in me] by word and deed through the might of signs and wonders, by the power of the Holy Spirit; so that from Jerusalem and as far around as Illyricum, I have fulfilled with abiding results*m* [my ministry in] the gospel of the Christ. [20]And in this manner it has always been my aim*n* to declare the good news where the name of Christ has not been uttered, so as not to build upon a foundation laid by another workman, [21]but as it stands written:

> Those who have not been told about him will see,
> And those who have not heard will understand.*o*

[22]This explains why I have so

---

*f*Objective genitive.
*g*Psalm 18:49.
*h*Deuteronomy 32:43.
*i*Psalm 117:1.
*j*Isaiah 11:10.
*k*Or, in some parts [of this letter].
*l*Subjective genitive.
*m*Force of *peplērōkenai*, perfect infinitive.
*n*Or, I consider it an honor.
*o*Isaiah 52:15.

frequently[p] been prevented by many responsibilities[q] from coming to you. 23But now, as I no longer have a place [of work] in these regions, and as I have for a good many years cherished a longing to come to you, 24I am hoping to see you when I pass through [Rome] on my way to Spain, and by you to be assisted on the journey there, after I have had the pleasure of your fellowship for a while. 25However, at the present I am going to Jerusalem for the purpose[r] of delivering the collection[s] to the saints. 26For [the churches of] Macedonia and Achaia have resolved to contribute a certain sum for the poor among the saints at Jerusalem. 27Indeed they were glad to do so, and actually the Gentiles[t] owe a debt to the Jews; for if the Gentiles have shared in their spiritual benefits, [the Gentiles] in fact ought to minister to them in material things. 28After I have completed this [task], and have properly delivered the contribution to them, I shall proceed toward Spain and visit you on the way. 29And I know that when I do reach you, I shall come in the fullness of Christ's blessing.

30Now I appeal to you, [my] brothers, through our Lord Jesus Christ, and by the love[u] which the Spirit[v] imparts, to agonize together with me in your prayers to God in my behalf, 31that I may be delivered from those persons in Judea who are disobedient, and that my service which takes me to Jerusalem may be well received by the saints; 32so that, by the will of God, I may come to you with gladness and enjoy [a period of] refreshing rest in your company. 33May the God of peace be with all of you! Amen.

Chapter 16

Now I commend to you our sister Phoebe, who is a servant[a] of the church at Cenchreae. 2Receive her in the Lord, in the manner in which saints should welcome one another. Stand by her in whatever matter she may have need of you, for indeed she on her part has rendered much assistance to many, including myself.

3Give my greetings to Prisca and Aquila, my fellow workers in Christ Jesus. 4They once risked their own lives in behalf of mine. Not only I but also all the churches of the Gentiles give thanks to them. 5[Greet], too, the church which meets in their house. Greet my beloved Epaenetus, who is the first convert won for Christ in [the province of] Asia. 6Greet Mary, who has toiled a great deal for you. 7Greet Andronicus and Junias, my fellow countrymen, who also shared imprisonment with me; they are men of esteem among the apostles, and they have been in Christ longer than I. 8Greet Ampliatus, my beloved in

---

[p]Implied by imperfect tense of verb.

[q]Literally, "many things."

[r]Force of present participle, *diakonōn.*

[s]Greek, "ministering to the saints." Collection is indicated by context.

[t]Greek, "they are debtors of them."

[u]*Agapē.*

[v]Subjective genitive.

[a]Or, deacon. The Greek word, *diakonos,* is common gender.

the Lord. [9]Give my greetings to Urbanus, our fellow worker in Christ, and to my beloved Stachys. [10]Greet Apelles, that man of tested character in [the work of] Christ. Greet those of the [household] of Aristobulus. [11]Greet Herodion, my fellow countryman. Greet those of the [household] of Narcissus who are in the Lord. [12]Greet Tryphaena and Tryphosa, those diligent toilers in [the cause of] the Lord. Greet Persis, the beloved lady who, with regard to many things, has worked hard for the Lord.[b] [13]Greet Rufus, that excellent man in the Lord; also his mother—[she has been a mother] to me too. [14]Greet Asyncritus, Phlegon, Hermes, Patrobas, Hermas, and the brothers who are associated with them. [15]Greet Philologus and Julia, Nereus and his sister, and Olympas, and all the saints who are associated with them. [16]Greet one another with a holy kiss. All the churches of the Christ send their greetings to you.

[17]Now I urge you, [my] brothers, to keep on the lookout for those persons who create divisions and means of entrapment. [Their teachings are] contrary to the doctrine which you[c] have learned. [18]Keep away from them, for such men are not obedient to our Lord Christ, but to their own selfish appetite, and by means of their smooth speech and flattering

style they deceive completely the hearts of the credulous. [19]The report of your obedience [to the truth] has reached everyone; so I rejoice on account of you, yet I want you to be wise with reference to what is good, but untainted with reference to what is evil. [20]The God of peace will crush Satan under your feet swiftly. The gracious care of our Lord Jesus [be][d] with you!

[21]Timothy, my fellow worker, greets you, and [so do] Lucius and Jason and Sosipater, my fellow countrymen. [22](I, Tertius, who served as amanuensis[e] for this epistle, greet you in the Lord.) [23]Gaius, my host, and [host] of the entire church, greets you. Erastus, the administrator[f] of the city, and Brother Quartus, greet you.

[25][g]Now to him who is able to establish you in accord with the gospel as I preach it,[h] even the proclamation of Jesus Christ, in accord with the disclosure of the mystery which was kept in a state of silence during long ages, [26]but now has been made plain through prophetic scriptures [and], by the command of the eternal God, made known to all the Gentiles to bring them to the obedience which faith[i] impels—[27]to God [who] alone [is] wise, to whom through Jesus Christ be glory forever![j] Amen.

---

[b]Literally, in the Lord.
[c]Emphatic *humeis*.
[f]Or, treasurer.
[g]Nestle, following the best textual authorities, omits verse 24. But the benediction of the verse, almost word for word, is included in verse 20 by these sources.
[h]Literally, my gospel.
[i]Subjective genitive.

[d]Or, [is].
[e]Greek, "the one having written."

[j]Greek, "unto the ages of the ages."

References

Listed below are the publications to which references were made in the Preface and in Part I. Excerpts quoted are used by permission of the copyright owners, to whom acknowledgment is hereby made with gratitude.

Alford, Henry, *The New Testament for English Readers*. Chicago: Moody Press, n.d.

Barmby, J., et al, *The Epistle to the Romans* (The Pulpit Commentary). Grand Rapids: Wm. B. Eerdmans Publishing Company, 1950.

Barnett, Albert E., *The New Testament: Its Making and Meaning*. Revised Edition. New York and Nashville: Abingdon Press, 1958.

Breasted, James Henry, *Ancient Times: A History of the Early World*. Boston: Ginn and Company, 1916.

Bruce, F. F., *The Book of Acts* (The New International Commentary on the New Testament). Grand Rapids: Wm. B. Eerdmans Publishing Company, 1955.

Cartledge, Samuel A., *A Conservative Introduction to the New Testament*. Seventh Edition. Grand Rapids: Zondervan Publishing House, 1957.

Cullmann, Oscar, *Peter: Disciple—Apostle—Martyr* (Translated from the German by Floyd V. Filson). London: SCM Press Ltd. and Philadelphia: The Westminster Press, 1953.

Denney, James, *St. Paul's Epistle to the Romans* (The Expositor's Greek Testament). Grand Rapids: Wm. B. Eerdmans Publishing Company, n.d.

Dibelius, Martin, *A Fresh Approach to the New Testament and Early Christian Literature*. New York: Charles Scribner's Sons, 1936.

Dods, Marcus, *An Introduction to the New Testament*. London: Hodder and Stoughton, n.d.

Filson, Floyd V., *Pioneers of the Primitive Church*. New York: The Abingdon Press, 1940.

Goodspeed, Edgar J., *The Formation of the New Testament*. Chicago: The University of Chicago Press, 1926.

———, *An Introduction to the New Testament*. Chicago: The University of Chicago Press, 1937.

Hort, F. J. A., "On the End of the Epistle to the Romans," in J. B. Lightfoot. *Biblical Essays*. London and New York: Macmillan and Company, 1893.

Hunter, Archibald M., *Introducing the New Testament*. Second Edition. Philadelphia: The Westminster Press, 1957.

Knox, Ronald A., *The New Testament of our Lord and Saviour Jesus Christ: A New Translation*. New York: Sheed & Ward, 1947.

Knox, John and Cragg, Gerald R., *The Epistle to the Romans* (The Interpreter's Bible). New York and Nashville: Abingdon-Cokesbury Press, 1954.

Lake, Kirsopp (Translator), *The Apostolic Fathers* (Loeb Classical Library). Vol. I. Cambridge: Harvard University Press, 1949.

———, *Eusebius: The Ecclesiastical History* (Loeb Classical Library). Vol. I. New York: G. P. Putnam's Sons, 1926.

Laubach, Frank C., *The Inspired Letters in Clearest English.* New York: Thomas Nelson & Sons, 1956.

Lenski, R. C. H., *The Interpretation of St. Paul's Epistle to the Romans.* Columbus: Wartburg Press, 1945. Quotations used by permission of Augsburg Publishing House, present copyright holder.

Lightfoot, J. B., *Biblical Essays.* London and New York: Macmillan and Company, 1893.

McCasland, S. Vernon, "The Greco-Roman World," in *The Interpreter's Bible,* Vol. VII. New York and Nashville: Abingdon-Cokesbury Press, 1951.

Merk, Augustinus, *Novum Testamentum Graece et Latine.* Editio quinta. Roma: Sumptibus Pontificii Instituti Biblici, 1944.

Moffatt, James, *The New Testament: A New Translation.* New York: Richard R. Smith, Inc., 1930. Copyright by James Moffatt, 1954. Quotations used by permission of Harper and Brothers.

Moule, Handley C. G., *The Epistle to the Romans.* London: Pickering and Inglis Ltd., n.d.

Nestle, Eberhard, *Hē Kainē Diathēkē.* London: British and Foreign Bible Society, 1934.

———, and Erwin Nestle, *Novum Testamentum Graece.* Editio quinta decima. Stuttgart: Privilegierte Württembergische Bibelanstalt, 1932.

Phillips, J. B., *Letters to Young Churches: A Translation of the New Testament Epistles.* New York: The Macmillan Company, 1951.

———, *The New Testament in Modern English.* New York: The Macmillan Company, 1958.

Roberts, Alexander and Donaldson, James (editors), *The Ante-Nicene Fathers.* American reprint of the Edinburgh edition. Revised by A. Cleveland Coxe. Vol. I. Grand Rapids: Wm. B. Eerdmans Publishing Company, n.d.

Robertson, A. T., *A Grammar of the Greek New Testament in the Light of Historical Research.* Fifth Edition. New York: Harper and Brothers, 1931. Quotations used by permission of Broadman Press, present copyright holder.

———, *Word Pictures in the New Testament.* Vol. IV. Nashville: Broadman Press, 1931.

Sanday, William and Headlam, Arthur C., *The Epistle to the Romans* (The International Critical Commentary). Eleventh Edition. New York: Charles Scribner's Sons, 1906.

Schonfield, Hugh J., *The Authentic New Testament.* New York: The New American Library of World Literature, Inc., 1958.

Scott, Ernest Findlay, *The Literature of the New Testament.* New York: Columbia University Press, 1932.

Stifler, James M., *The Epistle to the Romans: A Commentary Logical and Historical.* Chicago: Moody Press, 1960.

Taylor, William M., *Paul the Missionary.* New York: Richard R. Smith, Inc., 1930. Quotations used by permission of Harper and Brothers.

Thiessen, Henry Clarence, *Introduction to the New Testament.* Grand Rapids: Wm. B. Eerdmans Publishing Company, 1958.

Williams, Charles B., *The New Testament: A Translation in the Language of the People.* Chicago: Moody Press, 1949.

INDICES FOR PART I

Index of Persons and Subjects

Index of Scripture Texts